LIVING THROUGH THE END OF THE COLD WAR

LIVING THROUGH THE END OF THE COLD WAR

LIVING THROUGH THE END OF THE COLD WAR

Edited by Jeff Hay

Bruce Glassman, *Vice President*
Bonnie Szumski, *Publisher*
Helen Cothran, *Managing Editor*
Scott Barbour, *Series Editor*

GREENHAVEN PRESS
An imprint of Thomson Gale, a part of The Thomson Corporation

THOMSON
—★—
GALE

Detroit • New York • San Francisco • San Diego • New Haven, Conn.
Waterville, Maine • London • Munich

LIBRARY OF CONGRESS CATALOGING-IN-PUBLICATION DATA

Living through the end of the Cold War / Jeff Hay, book editor.
    p. cm. — (Living through the Cold War)
    Includes bibliographical references and index.
    ISBN 0-7377-2132-4 (lib: alk. paper)
    1. History, Modern—1989– . 2. History, Modern—1989—Sources. 3. World politics—1989– . 4. World politics—1989—Sources. 5. Soviet Union—Politics and government—1985–1991. 6. Soviet Union—Politics and government—1985–1991—Sources. 7. Europe, Eastern—History—1989– . I. Hay, Jeff. II. Series.

D860.L58 2005
940.55'8—dc22   2004042437

Printed in the United States of America

Chapter 1: Speeches and Writings from Leaders

Chapter 2: Life Under Glasnost and Perestroika

Chapter 3: The Iron Curtain Comes Down

At the midpoint of the Cold War, in early 1968, U.S. television viewers saw surprising reports from Vietnam, where American ground troops had been fighting since 1965. They learned that South Vietnamese Communist rebels, known as the Vietcong, had attacked unexpectedly throughout the country. At one point Vietcong insurgents engaged U.S. troops and officials in a firefight at the very center of U.S. power in Vietnam, the American embassy in South Vietnam's capital, Saigon. Meanwhile, thousands of soldiers and marines faced a concerted siege at Khe Sanh, an isolated base high in central Vietnam's mountains. Their adversary was not the Vietcong, but rather the regular North Vietnamese army.

Reporters and U.S. citizens quickly learned that these events constituted the Tet Offensive, a coordinated attack by Vietnamese Communists that occurred in late January, the period of Tet, Vietnam's new year. The American public was surprised by the Tet Offensive because they had been led to believe that the United States and its South Vietnamese allies were winning the war, that Vietcong forces were weak and dwindling, and that the massive buildup of American forces (there were some five hundred thousand U.S. troops in Vietnam by early 1968), ensured that the south would remain free of a Communist takeover. Since 1965, politicians, pundits, and generals had claimed that massive American intervention was justified and that the war was being won. On a publicity tour in November 1967 General William Westmoreland, the American commander in Vietnam, had assured officials and reporters that "the ranks of the Vietcong are thinning steadily" and that "we have reached a point where the end begins to come into view." President Lyndon B. Johnson's advisers, meanwhile, continually encouraged him to publicly emphasize "the light at the end of the tunnel."

Ordinary Americans had largely supported the troop build-up in Vietnam, believing the argument that the country was an important front in the Cold War, the global effort to stop the spread of communism that had begun in the late 1940s. Communist regimes already held power in nearby China, North Korea, and in northern Vietnam; it was deemed necessary to hold the line in the south not only to prevent communism from taking hold there but to prevent other nations from falling to communism throughout Asia. In 1965, polls showed that 80 percent of Americans believed that intervention in Vietnam was justified despite the fact that involvement in this fight would alter American life in numerous ways. For example, young men faced the possibility of being drafted and sent to fight—and possibly die—in a war thousands of miles away. As the war progressed, citizens watched more and more of their sons—both draftees and enlisted men—being returned to the United States in coffins (approximately fifty-eight thousand Americans died in Vietnam). Antiwar protests roiled college campuses and sometimes the streets of major cities. The material costs of the war threatened domestic political reforms and America's economic health, offering the continuing specter of rising taxes and shrinking services. Nevertheless, as long as the fight was succeeding, a majority of Americans could accept these risks and sacrifices.

Tet changed many minds, suggesting as it did that the war was not, in fact, going well. When CBS news anchor Walter Cronkite, who was known as "the most trusted man in America," suggested in his broadcast on the evening of February 27 that the Vietnam War might be unwinnable and could only end in a stalemate, many people wondered if he might be right and began to suspect that the positive reports from generals and politicians might have been misleading. It was a turning point in the battle for public opinion. Johnson reportedly said that Cronkite's expressions of doubt signaled the loss of mainstream America's support for the war. Indeed, after Tet more and more people joined Cronkite in wondering whether fighting this obscure enemy in an isolated country halfway around the world was worth the cost—whether it was a truly important front in the Cold War. They made their views known through demonstrations and opinion polls, and politicians were forced to respond. In a dramatic and unexpected turn of events, Johnson declined to run for reelection in 1968, stating that his involvement in the political campaign would detract from his efforts to negotiate a peace agreement with North Vietnam. His successor, Richard Nixon, won the election after promising to end the war.

The Tet Offensive and its consequences provide strong examples of how the Cold War touched the lives of ordinary Americans. Far from being an abstract geopolitical event, the Cold War, as Tet reveals, was an ever-present influence in the everyday life of the nation. Greenhaven Press's Living Through the Cold War series provides snapshots into the lives of ordinary people during the Cold War, as well as their reactions to its major events and developments. Each volume is organized around a particular event or distinct stage of the Cold War. Primary documents such as eyewitness accounts and speeches give firsthand insights into both ordinary peoples' experiences and leaders' decisions. Secondary sources provide factual information and place events within a larger global and historical context. Additional resources include a detailed introduction, a comprehensive chronology, and a thorough bibliography. Also included are an annotated table of contents and a detailed index to help the reader locate information quickly. With these features, the Living Through the Cold War series reveals the human dimension of the superpower rivalry that defined the globe during most of the latter half of the twentieth century.

On November 10, 1989, crowds rushed into the streets of Berlin, a German city divided since the late 1940s into free western and Communist eastern sides. Their intention was to break down the Berlin Wall, which Communist officials had built in 1961 and which suddenly had become irrelevant on November 9, when East German officials opened borders to West Germany. Champagne corks flew, people cried and shouted for joy, revelers linked arms and danced atop the wall or carried away chunks of it as souvenirs, and half-believing East Berliners stepped across the crumbling wall to the west, surprised by the variety of goods available in the shops. It was the remarkable climax of a remarkable few years and it heralded the end of the Cold War.

The Cold War, the ideological struggle that dominated the second half of the twentieth century, came to an abrupt and unexpected end two years later with the collapse of the Soviet Union. This collapse, made memorable by images of Russian president Boris Yeltsin facing down tanks in Moscow during an attempted coup by Communist hard-liners in August 1991, brought to a close two eventful years during which Communist regimes were overthrown across Eastern Europe, often by ordinary people no longer willing to accept the restrictions of Communist rule. The fall of the Berlin Wall remains the most indelible symbol of this transformation.

Hard-Line Opposition to Communism

While "people power" was indeed a major force behind the end of the Cold War, the foundation for these changes was laid by a string of remarkable leaders who first appeared on the international stage in 1980. They included Polish labor leader Lech Walesa, Czechoslovakian playwright Vaclav Havel, and Russian politician Boris Yeltsin. Yet future historians will probably look foremost to two figures when they examine the end of the Cold War: Ronald Reagan, president of the United States from January 1981 to January 1989, and Mikhail Gorbachev, general secretary of the Soviet Communist Party (and therefore leader of the Soviet Union) from March 1985 to December 1991.

When Reagan was elected president in 1980, few would have predicted that he would play a major role in bringing the Cold War to a close. Reagan was considered a representative of the far right wing of the Republican Party, a "hawk" with regard to the Soviet Union who seemed to favor confrontation rather than diplomacy. Indeed, for the first few years of his term in office Reagan played the role of a staunch cold warrior with great energy. He strongly criticized the Soviet invasion of Afghanistan, begun in 1979, as a new example of Communist intentions to dominate the world, and he encouraged the free nations of the West to take a powerful stand against this threat. In a March 1983 speech Reagan famously called the Soviet Union an "evil empire,"[1] a phrase that dramatically reflected the tone of his first term in office. He opposed efforts in the United States and Western Europe to mount a "nuclear freeze," or end to the production of nuclear weapons, which he maintained would give the Soviets an edge in the ongoing struggle between good and evil. Indeed, Reagan began anew the arms race between West and East that had stalled in the 1970s, ready to revive the American armed forces not only with more nuclear weapons and more troops but with new, fantastically conceived military technology.

For his efforts Reagan was labeled a cowboy and a loose cannon by many Europeans, although counterparts such as conservative British prime minister Margaret Thatcher tied themselves closely to his way of thinking. As an approach to foreign relations, Reagan and Thatcher approved of negotiation from a position of military strength, not one of weakness. Even during Reagan's second term, when he was engaged in arms control talks with Gorbachev, the president reminded the world of the nature of the Communist regimes and the Cold War when he made a 1987 visit to Berlin. There he sternly demanded to loud cheers, "Mr. Gorbachev, tear down this wall!"[2]

Signs of change, however, had already begun to appear behind the "iron curtain" that divided free Western and Communist Eastern Europe. In Poland in 1980, shipyard workers in the city of Gdansk staged strikes against higher food prices and soon formed a labor movement known as Solidarity. A worker named Lech Walesa rose to be the leader of Solidarity, a movement viewed as a threat by both the Polish and Soviet governments because it insisted on independence from the state and greater religious freedom, both anathema to Communist regimes. Walesa and Solidarity captured the attention of the world, and by July 1981 the movement had the support of a substantial portion of the ruling Polish Central Committee. With the moral support of the Soviets, however, and with implied threats of a Soviet military crackdown, the Polish government declared martial law in December 1981 and Walesa and other Solidarity leaders such as writer Adam Michnik were thrown in prison.

Radical Reform of the Communist State

In hindsight, the crackdown against Solidarity was the last gasp of decades of Communist repression in Eastern Europe. Leadership changes in the Soviet Union were to inspire fundamental changes behind the iron curtain; indeed, a generational shift was under way. When Reagan took office Leonid Brezhnev was the Soviet leader; he had held the position since 1964. Brezhnev died in November 1982 and was replaced by Yuri Andropov, another old-guard Soviet bureaucrat. Hopes for reforms under Andropov, whose tastes and sympathies seemed to be Western and who expressed interest in arms control talks, came to little, and the aging premier died in January 1984. The new Soviet leader was Konstantin Chernenko, another elderly relic of earlier days who died in office fourteen months later. The rapid succession of leadership left openings for a younger generation of leaders to rise to influential positions, most notably Mikhail Gorbachev. Gorbachev, who had become a member of the ruling Soviet Politburo under Andropov, quickly acquired a reputation both inside and outside the Soviet Union as a reform-minded

The Former Soviet Union

thinker. During his visit to Great Britain in January 1984, Thatcher proclaimed him to be a "communist [she could] do business with."[3]

Gorbachev rose to the position of general secretary upon Chernenko's death in March 1985. He arrived with relatively radical ideas intended to reform the Communist state and revive it after the stagnation of the Brezhnev era. Two Russian words became associated with Gorbachev's reforms: *perestroika*, meaning restructuring, and *glasnost*, which was usually translated as openness. Perestroika, primarily directed at the Soviet economy and bureaucracy, opened the door to certain democratic reforms. Restructuring was necessary, Gorbachev proclaimed, because the Soviet Union needed to give its people a higher standard of living and spur them to compete with the fast-developing technology and consumer economy of the West. To achieve these ends Gorbachev began to introduce free-market reforms into the closed Soviet economy, allowing, for example, independent entrepreneurs to operate their own small businesses such as restaurants or sales stalls.

Glasnost, openness, was to be broadly understood as greater honesty in political and cultural matters. Gorbachev was concerned that Soviet citizens' lack of trust and participation in government had produced in them a narrow, apathetic outlook that was inappropriate in an age of global communications and a threat to the survival of communism. He claimed that "wide, prompt, and frank information is evidence of confidence in the people and respect for their intelligence and feelings, and for their ability to understand events for themselves. It enhances the resourcefulness of the working people."[4] In functional terms glasnost often meant greater freedom of the press. Its effects were tangible: From 1985, ordinary Soviets took an energetic interest in expressing their concerns, hopes, and complaints in a growing body of newspapers and periodicals. Significantly, many of their comments were highly critical of the privations and restrictions of Soviet society, ranging from shoddy, hard-to-find consumer goods to the lack of decent housing. On another level glasnost was to include moves toward democratization, such as allowing local elections.

Partly because of his willingness to embrace social openness, and partly because his changes seemed to be a response to the American arms buildup, Gorbachev proved to be a Communist whom Reagan as well as Thatcher could do business with. In December 1984, shortly after Reagan was reelected in a landslide, American secretary of state George Schultz met with Soviet foreign minister Andrei Gromyko in Geneva, Switzerland. This ended three years of cold silence between the top officials of the two governments. A Geneva summit between Reagan and Gorbachev themselves followed in October 1985. Among their major priorities was renewing the arms limitation negotiations that had stalled in the late 1970s.

Historic Negotiations

In partial contrast to his reputation as an unrepentant hawk, Reagan was greatly concerned about the possibility of a nuclear confrontation, and he was willing to take reasonable risks to reduce such a possibility. He was ready to negotiate with Gorbachev on matters ranging from the placement of nuclear missiles in Europe to reducing total numbers of weapons on both sides. He was unwilling to compromise, however, on the matter of the so-called Strategic Defense Initiative (SDI). This

President Ronald Reagan and Soviet leader Mikhail Gorbachev meet for the first time during the 1985 Geneva summit.

plan, first proposed during his first term, involved the construction of a defensive shield over the United States in the form of such high-tech wizardry as satellites and lasers. Dubbed "Star Wars" by the media, SDI would, theoretically, make it impossible for a nuclear missile to strike the United States; any such weapon would be destroyed or disabled long before it reached the earth. Government agencies and defense contractors had already begun experimenting with SDI by the time Reagan met with Gorbachev in 1985, although many scientists doubted its feasibility and others criticized its high costs. In any case, Reagan committed himself to the concept, hopeful that the technology would make nuclear war impossible. He made it clear, moreover, that he was willing to share SDI technology with the Soviets as well as the nervous leaders of Western Europe. Gorbachev, however, considered Reagan's insistence on SDI a sticking point that amounted to an intention to assert American military superiority, and the Geneva summit ended inconclusively. Nevertheless, the two leaders had begun to build a relationship.

The second summit between Reagan and Gorbachev took place in Reykjavik, the capital of Iceland, in October 1986. It proved to be a major turning point. Both leaders made dramatic promises: to work for the elimination of intermediate-range nuclear missiles in Europe and to eliminate intercontinental ballistic missiles within ten years. Reagan offered to drop submarines and bomber aircraft as nuclear delivery systems, while Gorbachev pledged to substantially cut the size of the Soviet armed forces. Although the Reykjavik summit produced no detailed, enforceable agreement, advisers on both sides were shocked by the speed at which Reagan and Gorbachev moved. The Soviet leader later remembered that "Reykjavik marked a turning point in world history. It tangibly demonstrated that the world could be improved,"[5] showing how leaders could remove the nuclear threat that had hung over humankind since 1945.

The rapid changes in superpower relations even encouraged Reagan to temper his insistence on SDI, and in December 1987 he allowed the program's funding to be cut. Shortly afterward Gorbachev arrived in Washington, D.C., for the first-ever visit to the American capital by a Soviet leader. During the meetings the two leaders made further progress on arms limitation agreements, but the Washington summit was also memorable for its public relations impact. A wave of "Gorbymania" swept the United States as Gorbachev received a wide and enthusiastic welcome. An astute politician, Gorbachev took advantage of the warm reception, meeting with ordinary Americans and disarmingly wading into crowds in the streets with his sophisticated, attractive wife, Raisa, at his side. It seemed to many people that Gorbachev indeed represented a huge thaw in Cold War tensions. Not only was Soviet society opening up, and not only was Gorbachev freeing thousands of political prisoners and dissidents, he was working with the conservative U.S. president to eliminate the nuclear threat. Reagan followed the gesture with a visit to Moscow for a fourth summit in May 1988, where he in turn was warmly welcomed by ordinary Soviet citizens.

The Disintegration of the Communist Bloc

In December 1988, in a speech before the United Nations in New York City, Gorbachev pledged to make good on his promise to reduce Soviet armed forces and, furthermore, to withdraw most Soviet forces from the Eastern European Communist satellite states. A major reason for the continued existence of those regimes in the face of persistent protests was the specter of direct intervention by the Soviet army should the regimes falter, as was the case in 1981 with the crackdown of Solidarity in Poland. But Gorbachev promised to, in effect, end the threat of a Soviet crackdown, claiming that "force, or the threat of force, neither can nor should be instruments of foreign policy."[6] Encouraged, popular leaders and dissidents began to test Gorbachev, exploiting the tears and rips that began to occur in the iron curtain. Now freed from prison, Lech Walesa convinced the Polish government to allow free elections in June 1989. Solidarity won easily, and Walesa was given a prominent place in the new government. Hungarian Communists relaxed border restrictions between Hungary and free Austria, a step that allowed thousands of Hungarians, East Germans, and others to walk to freedom. When East German Commmunist leader Erich Honecker closed his borders and asked for Soviet help to stem the growing exodus, Gorbachev refused him. Sensing that change was inevitable and sincere in his belief that force could not be used in foreign relations, Gorbachev told Honecker that "life itself punishes those who delay,"[7] implying that Honecker should be prepared to accept reforms and that it was too late to resist. In late October 1989 Honecker was forced from power. Then, on November 10, sure that their actions would not put them in danger from Communist police or soldiers, the people of East and West Berlin tore down the wall that had divided their city since 1961.

November 1989 also saw the Velvet Revolution, which ended communism in Czechoslovakia. Following demonstrations by thousands of students, workers, and other ordinary citizens, the Communist government of Czechoslovakia was forced, without violence, to step down in favor of democratic replacements. Czechoslovakia had always enjoyed the political participation of artists and writers, but still the world was surprised when Vaclav Havel, a dissident playwright who openly called for a new era of peace and tolerance, was elected president of the new Czechoslovak Republic on December 29, 1989. It was a remarkable end to a year that Brent Scowcroft, national security adviser to new U.S. president George H.W. Bush, had opened by declaiming that "the Cold War is not over."[8] Events, it seemed, were moving too quickly for the new American administration to absorb.

The Disintegration of the Soviet Union

Meanwhile Gorbachev, by refusing to prop up the Communist regimes of Eastern Europe, inspired various ethnic groups within the Soviet Union to follow the model set by the Poles, East Germans, and Czechoslovakians. The Soviet Union had been assembled from the nineteenth-century Russian empire whose dominant group, the Russians, controlled various ethnic minorities including the Georgians, Ukrainians, Armenians, Azerbaijanis, and the Baltic peoples of Lithuania, Latvia, and Estonia. Now ethnic nationalism reasserted itself: By 1991 ethnic unrest was widespread throughout Gorbachev's domains and threatened to lead to open rebellion and warfare in some areas. The Baltic states boldly declared independence, daring the Soviets to react, but Moscow was helpless to stop the momentum of independence. Gorbachev was also beset by economic problems that perestroika had yet to fully address, troubles that were worsened by a global recession that set in in 1990. Although the Soviet leader won the Nobel Peace Prize in 1990, he faced increasing unpopularity at home.

Another of Gorbachev's generation of Soviet reformers, the popular Boris Yeltsin, was the president of the Russian Soviet Republic in 1991. He rose to global prominence when, in August of that year, Communist hard-liners tried to mount a coup against Gorbachev and return their nation to a version of its more totalitarian past. With Gorbachev forced by a "medical emergency" to retreat to a Russian resort area, Yeltsin was the leader on the spot when the hard-liners made their intentions known early on the morning of August 19. Anticipating such a move, Yeltsin was prepared to establish a Russian government in exile, but first he climbed atop a tank in front of the Russian parliament building in Moscow and exhorted Russians to disavow the coup and stage a general strike. Various miscalculations and blunders by the coup's plotters, not simply Yeltsin's courageous actions, led to the failure of the attempted coup. The world, however, remembered the news footage of Yeltsin as he faced down elements of the Soviet armed forces and entrenched bureaucracy, and he was hailed as the hero of the hour.

The Soviet Union did not last long after the botched coup attempt of August 1991. Gorbachev himself, still a dedicated Communist who wanted to preserve the Soviet Union, found himself marginalized as the world changed around him, and Yeltsin became the dominant leader in Russia. In cooperation with the leaders of breakaway republics, Yeltsin established the Confederation of Independent States, most of which hoped to move quickly from communism, a discredited ideology thanks to decades of totalitarianism, to democracy and the free market.

The Cold War, therefore, ended with more of a whimper than a bang, while the United States appeared to some to take the role of observer; in the opinion of Polish dissident Adam Michnik, the United States seemed to be "sleepwalking through history."[9] Especially in the period from 1989 to 1991 the turn of events was dizzying. But the remarkable leaders of both East and West, notably Gorbachev and Reagan, set the process in motion and actively shepherded change. Despite their very different ideologies and politics, and despite their missteps, they were able to overcome their suspicions and work together to lessen the Cold War threats and nuclear tensions that had threatened the world for decades.

Notes

1. Quoted in Martin Walker, *Cold War: A History*. New York: Henry Holt, 1993, p. 268.
2. Ronald Reagan, remarks at the Brandenburg Gate, West Berlin, Germany, June 12, 1987. Reagan Foundation, www.reaganfoundation.org/reagan/speeches/wall.asp.
3. Quoted in Walker, *Cold War*, p. 283.
4. Quoted in Walker, *Cold War*, pp. 283–84.
5. Quoted in Walker, *Cold War*, p. 293.
6. Mikhail Gorbachev, speech before the UN General Assembly, December 8, 1988.
7. Quoted in Benjamin Frankel, ed., "Mikhail Gorbachev," *The Cold War, 1945–1991*, vol. 2. Detroit: Gale Research, 1992, p. 116.
8. Quoted in Walker, *Cold War*, pp. 209–10.
9. Quoted in Walker, *Cold War*, p. 311.

CHAPTER 1

Speeches and Writings from Leaders

The Soviet Union Wants Peace and Cooperation

Mikhail Gorbachev

Even before he became the general secretary of the Soviet Communist Party in March 1985 and therefore the Soviet leader, Mikhail Gorbachev began to gain a reputation outside his own country as an innovator who recognized the need for internal change and also as a rising star within the inner Soviet ruling circle. The following selection is from a speech Gorbachev gave to the British Parliament in December 1984. During the visit British prime minister Margaret Thatcher, a staunch Cold Warrior and close ally of U.S. president Ronald Reagan, declared that Gorbachev "was a communist [she] could work with." The admission was striking, since the trend in relations between the Soviet Union and the Western allies in 1983 and 1984 was toward increased tension over such issues as arms expansion and international influence.

Gorbachev used his speech to remind British leaders that the Soviet Union was interested in seeking peace, and he took the opportunity to include a veiled jibe at the United States, which had recently alarmed Soviet leaders by engaging in a broad military exercise known as "Able Archer," which some leaders thought signaled preparations for armed conflict. But his larger themes were the inevitable common destiny of the nations of Europe and the need, in an age of nuclear weapons, to build relations between

Mikhail Gorbachev, address to the British Parliament, December 18, 1984.

countries on a basis of realism. The speech was very well received by both Parliament and the British press.

Hardly anyone will deny the fact that the destinies of the nations of Europe are indivisible; they were such when Europe lived in peace and accord and when storm clouds swept low over its lands. Profoundly convinced of this, we have come to your country with the intention of discussing what can be done by our two countries and their parliaments to ameliorate Soviet-British relations and improve the international situation as a whole. How the future of mankind and relations between individual states and groups of countries will shape depends on the concrete steps that are undertaken or may be undertaken today on the problems of war and peace and international co-operation.

These questions were in the focus of our discussions with the Prime Minister, Mrs. Thatcher, the Foreign Secretary, Sir Geoffrey Howe, and other cabinet members. The exchange of opinion was businesslike, frank and, in our view, useful. Now, speaking before the members of the British Parliament, I would like in the first place to express what we think important for improving the international situation and developing our bilateral relations.

It is well known that in the seventies Europe became the cradle of the policy of détente [a "release" of Cold War tensions]. At that time important lines of co-operation formed between the countries of Western Europe on the one hand and the Soviet Union and other socialist countries on the other. That process was joined by the United States and Canada who both signed the Helsinki Final Act [a recognition of the Soviet sphere in Eastern Europe].

Reducing the Nuclear Threat

At one time it became possible to stop the channels of proliferation of nuclear weapons. That was formalized in the relevant international Treaty on the Non-Proliferation of Nuclear Weapons, to which more than 100 states are party today. Nuclear weapons tests in the atmosphere, outer space and under water were ended and banned, and talks were in progress on a general and complete prohibition of such tests. As a result of Soviet-American agreements, definite limitations were imposed on strategic nuclear arms and anti-missile defence systems. Active measures were under way to seek possible means of scaling down the arms race in other directions—both weapons of mass destruction and in conventional arms. The political dialogue was gathering momentum. Trade relations, cultural, scientific and other exchanges became appreciably more active. Nobody can deny the obvious fact that in the years to détente people felt safer and had greater confidence in their future.

In short, a normalization of the international climate was in evidence. It was not based on concessions by one side to the other. It was an expression of realism based on consideration of the mutual interests of countries belonging to different social systems and a general awareness of the fact that one's own security cannot be founded on means that prejudice the security of others.

In other words, it was a victory for common sense and a realization of the fact that war is an unfit and unacceptable method of settling disputes and that in a nuclear war, as in arms race and confrontation, there can be no winners. It had become obvious that the Cold War was an abnormal state of relations constantly fraught with the risk of war. All this had laid the groundwork for the favourable trend of international events in the seventies. On this foundation the peaceful coexistence of states belonging to different social systems became more and more deeply and securely implanted in the entire system of international relations. We believe that today, too, no reasonable alternative to the policy of peaceful coexistence exists or can exist. I wish to lay strong emphasis on this fact.

The Tension of the Early 1980s

One naturally wonders why there has been a new increase in the danger of war when it was possible at that time to lessen it. I shall not go into details. The Soviet viewpoint on this subject is well known. Nevertheless, I wish to say once again that the cause of that change for the worse—which is corroborated by facts—was a change in the policy of certain forces seeking to achieve military superiority and thereby gain the ability to dictate their will to others.

We in the Soviet Union well remember the statements and actions that created the climate of mistrust and hostility and led to a destabilization of the international situation. However, I am recalling this today without meaning to give offence to anybody.

We see our aim in deciding jointly—since nobody can do it alone—the most important problems which are essentially common to all of us: how to prevent war; how to check the arms race and proceed to disarmament; how to settle existing, and prevent potential, conflicts and crises; how to create a world situation that would allow every country to concentrate its attention and resources on solving its own problems (just name a country where no problems exist); how to pool efforts to deal with global problems—the fight against famine and disease, protection of the environment, provision of mankind with energy and raw material resources.

If Great Britain abides by this approach, we would be glad to co-operate with it. If the United States abides by the same approach and really puts its policy on the lines of peaceful co-operation, it, too, will find a dependable partner in us.

This is how we see the situation, and it is with these views that our parliamentary delegation has come to Britain.

If one agrees with the basic principles I have listed, the main question will still remain: how to solve the problems all of us consider important, how to prevent a further deterioration of the current dangerous situation and achieve a stable and secure situation in the world. In other words, how to lessen tensions, to clear the debris of Cold War and to revive détente, fruitful negotiations and co-operation.

For that, words alone are not enough (although they are also important in politics). Concrete action is necessary. A practical solution, if you will, to outstanding problems is required. As we see it, it is now important, as never before, for every country—its government, parliament, political and public circles—to be aware of its responsibility for the state of world affairs. We in the Soviet Union remember the horrors of the last war and clearly realize the catastrophic consequences of a future war; we are doing, and will do, our level best to live up to this great responsibility.

I will not list now all our foreign policy proposals and initiatives. I shall only say that they provide for as radical cuts in nuclear arms as possible (down to their complete elimination), as well as for cuts in conventional armaments, a ban on chemical weapons and the liquidation of stocks. We desire a broad dialogue and the development of mutually beneficial co-operation on a basis of equality in solving acute political problems, in the economic field, in science and technology, and in the area of cultural ties and exchanges.

Nuclear War Must Not Happen

When we speak of war and peace, we ought to keep it in mind that the character of modern weapons, nuclear weapons first and foremost, has changed the traditional concepts of these problems. Mankind is on the threshold of a new stage in the scientific and technological revolution, which will affect, in particular, the future development of military technology. Those who discourse on "limited," "short," or "protracted" nuclear wars are evidently still captives of the old-fashioned stereotypes of the time when war was a great tragedy but did not threaten mankind with extinction as it does today. The nuclear age inevitably dictates new political thinking. The most acute and urgent problem facing all people on earth today is the problem of averting nuclear war.

Our proposal for establishing definite rules of behaviour for the nuclear powers pursues the aim of averting the threat of nuclear war, finding a way to check the arms race, and to create a world situation where no nation would fear for its future. It will be recalled that the Soviet Union has already assumed a unilateral commitment not to use nuclear weapons first.

Such is our policy of principle. This is the starting point of all our proposals aimed at curbing the arms race and preventing war.

Guided by this principle, the Soviet Union has recently come forward with the initiative of holding talks with the United States on the full range of problems concerning nuclear and space weapons. On the basis of this initiative, agreement has been reached with the U.S. Administration to open a completely new round of talks covering both the problem of the non-militarization of outer space and that of the reduction of strategic and intermediate-range nuclear weapons. All of these should be discussed and settled as interlinked problems. Prevention of a race in space weapons is of key significance. Should such a race be started, it would not only be dangerous of itself but it would also whip up the arms race in other directions. The Soviet Union is prepared to seek and elaborate the most radical solutions to all these problems which would assist progress towards a total ban on nuclear weapons and eventually their complete elimination. It is now up to the United States, in its turn, to take a realistic stance that would facilitate the success of the negotiations.

We know that all issues concerning a lessening of the risk of nuclear war are widely discussed in Great Britain and other countries of Western Europe. The questions of defence and security are, of course, an internal affair of the sovereign states. I can declare, however, that any concrete step in the direction of lessening the risk of nuclear war, in Europe in particular, will find a corresponding practical response on our part.

It is true, of course, that the Soviet Union and Great Britain often take different stances on major international problems. Neither of us is playing down this fact. Nevertheless, it is our profound conviction that under present conditions all countries and peoples need, as never before, a constructive dialogue, a search for solutions to key international problems, for areas of agreement that could lead to greater mutual trust and create an international climate free from the nuclear menace, hostility and suspicion, fear and hatred.

Soviet Goals

The Soviet Union has formulated its approach in clear and unambiguous terms: to end tensions, to settle differences and disputed problems not by force or threats but through negotiations taking account of each other's legitimate interests, to avoid interference in each other's internal affairs. I would put it this way: all must constantly learn to live together, adapting to the realities of the modern world constantly changing in accordance with its own laws.

The development of the world situation is largely influenced by the way relations take shape between states in Europe. I have already mentioned the favourable trends in these relations in the seventies, especially after the adoption of the Final Act of the all-European conference at Helsinki. This document remains to this day a life-giving source, feeding the trends towards mutual understanding and co-operation in Europe, and not only in Europe. We believe that this source should be protected against bombardment and blockage.

Indeed, good relations between European states are largely a guarantee of security and peace in the world as a whole. The peoples of Europe have paid a high price for understanding that under no circumstances should one connive with forces that to this day persist in their attempts to revise the territorial realities that took shape in Europe in the wake of the Second World War. These realities were borne of a joint victory. They are reflected and affirmed in the inter-allied agreements on the postwar order, in important bilateral negotiations between a number of states, and in the Helsinki Final Act. Allegiance to all this must constitute a solid obstacle in the way of those who would like to call in question the results of the Second World War and postwar development, the inviolability of the state frontiers in Europe. There is no room for any ambiguities here. . . .

The Importance of Europe

I have listed just a few of the most vital problems whose solution would help put an end to the arms race and consolidate European and world security. I wish to emphasize again that the leadership of the Soviet Union are in favour of concrete and honest negotiations that would help make progress in solving, on a mutually acceptable basis, the problems involved in the limitation and reduction of armaments, especially nuclear weapons, right down to their complete elimination. We are prepared to meet our Western partners in negotiations halfway. Naturally, parity and equal security will have to be the basis for any arrangement. Needless to say, any move to achieve military superiority over the Soviet Union and its allies is unacceptable and would fail.

All of us are agreed that we live in a vulnerable, rather fragile but interconnected world. It is a world where coexistence is necessary, whether one wants it or not. Whatever divides us, we have the same planet to live on. Europe is our common home; and it is a home, not a "theatre of war".

The Soviet Union is in favour of normalizing relations between states. In politics and diplomacy there is always room enough for reasonable compromises, and a vast field for developing and strengthening mutual understanding and trust on a basis of similar or identical interests. It is the desire to cultivate this field that is needed. The Soviet Union and Great Britain, the Soviet and British peoples have such identical interests; the most important is the preservation of peace.

Steps Toward Greater Co-operation

The history of Soviet-British relations is more than sixty years old, and it has its own unforgettable milestones. In the postwar period there were years of productive co-operation. There were also times of decline. And today our relations, which are not developing in a political vacuum but in the troubled atmosphere of a growing nuclear danger, are not on the upgrade and are far from what is desirable. It will be recalled that at one time Britain was the Soviet Union's leading trade partner. Today it is no higher than seventh or eighth. I cannot but agree with the opinion of those representatives of Britain's trade and industrial circles who believe that politics should help commerce and commerce should promote mutual understanding and trust. This is absolutely correct.

British MPs [members of Parliament] know that a number of British statesmen have held talks in Moscow this year. We have declared our willingness to develop Soviet-British relations actively and on a wide range of questions. If the British side takes the same stance, this development will become a fact. May I avail myself of this opportunity to reaffirm this viewpoint of the Soviet Union.

The foreign policy of every state is inseparable from its home affairs, social and economic aims and requirements. The main aim of our plans is to advance considerably the material and cultural levels of the life of our people.

Our Party and State are directing their chief efforts to further economic developments by raising the efficiency of production and re-gearing the economy on the lines of intensification. Acceleration of scientific and technological progress in industry and agriculture is the focus of our work. We are setting and tackling large-scale and long-term tasks designed for the period up to the year 2000, taking advantage of all the achievements of the scientific and technological revolution available to man.

The Soviet Union needs peace to accomplish these truly breath-taking development plans. This is our policy of principle which is not dependent on any political expendiency. Great historical responsibility for the present and future of the world devolves today on its political leaders, legislators, on all those who shape the policies of states.

In view of this, the Supreme Soviet [ruling council] of the USSR, in its appeals of December 1982 and December 1983, clearly declared that the Soviet Union does not threaten the security of any country in the West or in the East. It desires to live at peace with all countries, to translate into reality the principles of peaceful coexistence of states belonging to different socio-political systems. The supreme legislative body of the USSR has expressed its willingness to make an effective contribution, jointly with the parliaments of other countries, to solving the most burning problem of today—that of saving mankind from nuclear catastrophe.

The world situation is truly complicated. The risk of war is one of today's realities. In the face of this grim reality I wish to emphasize this idea: let us look to the future and let us not forget the past. In other words, without forgetting what is good or bad, and learning lessons from both, let us concentrate all our efforts on opening new horizons for confident progress towards a world safer for all and truly secure.

Our delegation has been staying in Britain for a few days. We are grateful for the hospitality accorded us here and we hope that our visit, our new acquaintances and meetings will assist Soviet-British co-operation for the benefit of the peoples of our two countries, co-operation that will develop in the interest of mutual understanding and peace on earth.

May I avail myself of this opportunity to convey best wishes for prosperity, happiness and peace from the peoples of the Soviet Union to the people of Great Britain.

"Mr. Gorbachev, Tear Down This Wall!"

Ronald Reagan

The following selection is from a speech U.S. president Ronald Reagan made in West Berlin in June 1987. He made the speech near the Berlin Wall, the infamous barrier that had divided free West Berlin from Communist East Berlin since 1961. West Berlin, an enclave of democracy completely surrounded by Communist territory, had served throughout the Cold War as a symbol of freedom, and Reagan followed a number of presidents who had journeyed to the city to reiterate their intention to keep Berlin free. Although by 1987 he had begun to develop a strong working relationship with Soviet leader Mikhail Gorbachev that had led to discussions over arms limitation, among other matters, Reagan remained a strong Cold Warrior, as the speech indicates. The high point of his speech was his demand that Gorbachev, whom Reagan acknowledged as a reformer, "tear down this wall" in order to demonstrate his real commitment to progress.

We come to Berlin, we American presidents, because it's our duty to speak, in this place, of freedom. But I must confess, we're drawn here by other things as well: by the feeling of history in this city, more than 500 years older than our own nation; by the beauty of the Grunewald and the Tiergarten; most of all, by your courage and determination. Perhaps the composer Paul Lincke understood something about American presidents. You see, like so many presidents before me, I come here today because wherever I go, whatever I do:

Ronald Reagan, remarks at the Brandenburg Gate, West Berlin, Germany, June 12, 1987.

Ich hab' noch einen Koffer in Berlin [I still have a suitcase in Berlin].

Our gathering today is being broadcast throughout Western Europe and North America. I understand that it is being seen and heard as well in the East. To those listening throughout Eastern Europe, a special word: Although I cannot be with you, I address my remarks to you just as surely as to those standing here before me. For I join you, as I join your fellow countrymen in the West, in this firm, this unalterable belief: Es gibt nur ein Berlin [There is only one Berlin].

Behind me stands a wall that encircles the free sectors of this city, part of a vast system of barriers that divides the entire continent of Europe. From the Baltic, south, those barriers cut across Germany in a gash of barbed wire, concrete, dog runs, and guard towers. Farther south, there may be no visible, no obvious wall. But there remain armed guards and checkpoints all the same—still a restriction on the right to travel, still an instrument to impose upon ordinary men and women the will of a totalitarian state. Yet it is here in Berlin where the wall emerges most clearly; here, cutting across your city, where the news photo and the television screen have imprinted this brutal division of a continent upon the mind of the world. Standing before the Brandenburg Gate, every man is a German, separated from his fellow men. Every man is a Berliner, forced to look upon a scar.

[West German] President von Weizsäcker has said, "The German question is open as long as the Brandenburg Gate is closed." Today I say: As long as the gate is closed, as long as this scar of a wall is permitted to stand, it is not the German question alone that remains open, but the question of freedom for all mankind. Yet! do not come here to lament. For I find in Berlin a message of hope, even in the shadow of this wall, a message of triumph.

In this season of spring in 1945, the people of Berlin emerged from their air-raid shelters to find devastation. Thousands of miles away, the people of the United States reached out to help. And in 1947 Secretary of State . . . George Marshall announced the creation of what would become known as the Marshall Plan. Speaking precisely 40 years ago this month, he said: "Our policy is directed not against any country or doctrine, but against hunger, poverty, desperation, and chaos."

Building the Post–World War II West

In the Reichstag [German parliament building] a few moments ago, I saw a display commemorating this 40th anniversary of the Marshall Plan. I was struck by the sign on a burnt-out, gutted structure that was being rebuilt. I understand that Berliners of my own generation can remember seeing signs like it dotted throughout the western sectors of the city. The sign read simply: "The Marshall Plan is helping here to strengthen the free world." A strong, free world in the West, that dream became real. Japan rose from ruin to become an economic giant. Italy, France, Belgium—virtually every nation in Western Europe saw political and economic rebirth; the European Community was founded.

In West Germany and here in Berlin, there took place an economic miracle, the Wirtschaftswunder. Adenauer, Erhard, Reuter, and other leaders understood the practical importance of liberty—that just as truth can flourish only when the journalist is given freedom of speech, so prosperity can come about only when the farmer and businessman enjoy economic freedom. The German leaders reduced tariffs, expanded free trade, lowered taxes. From 1950 to 1960 alone, the standard of living in West Germany and Berlin doubled.

Where four decades ago there was rubble, today in West Berlin there is the greatest industrial output of any city in Germany—busy office blocks, fine homes and apartments, proud avenues, and the spreading lawns of parkland. Where a city's culture seemed to have been destroyed, today there are two great universities, orchestras and an opera, countless theaters, and museums. Where there was want, today there's abundance —food, clothing, automobiles—the wonderful goods of the Ku'damm [Berlin's main shopping street]. From devastation, from utter ruin, you Berliners have, in freedom, rebuilt a city that once again ranks as one of the greatest on earth. The Soviets may have had other plans. But my friends, there were a few things the Soviets didn't count on—Berliner Herz, Berliner

Humor, ja, und Berliner Schnauze [Berliner heart, Berliner humor, yes, and a Berliner Schnauze].

In the 1950s [Soviet premier Nikita] Khrushchev predicted: "We will bury you." But in the West today, we see a free world that has achieved a level of prosperity and well-being unprecedented in all human history. In the Communist world, we see failure, technological backwardness, declining standards of health, even want of the most basic kind—too little food. Even today, the Soviet Union still cannot feed itself. After these four decades, then, there stands before the entire world one great and inescapable conclusion: Freedom leads to prosperity. Freedom replaces the ancient hatreds among the nations with comity and peace. Freedom is the victor.

Calling on Gorbachev

And now the Soviets themselves may, in a limited way: be coming to understand the importance of freedom. We hear much from Moscow about a new policy of reform and openness. Some political prisoners have been released. Certain foreign news broadcasts are no longer being jammed. Some economic enterprises have been permitted to operate with greater freedom from state control.

Are these the beginnings of profound changes in the Soviet state? Or are they token gestures, intended to raise false hopes in the West, or to strengthen the Soviet system without changing it? We welcome change and openness; for we believe that freedom and security go together, that the advance of human liberty can only strengthen the cause of world peace. There is one sign Soviets can make that would be unmistakable, that would advance dramatically the cause of freedom and peace.

General Secretary Gorbachev, if you seek peace, if you seek prosperity for the Soviet Union and Eastern Europe, if you seek liberalization: Come here to this gate! Mr. Gorbachev, open this gate! Mr. Gorbachev, tear down this wall!

The Need to Stay Strong

I understand the fear of war and the pain of division that afflict this continent—and I pledge to you my country's efforts

Standing at the Brandenburg Gate, President Reagan challenged Soviet leader Mikhail Gorbachev to "Tear down this wall!"

to help overcome these burdens. To be sure, we in the West must resist Soviet expansion. So we must maintain defenses of unassailable strength. Yet we seek peace; so we must strive to reduce arms on both sides.

Beginning 10 years ago, the Soviets challenged the Western alliance with a grave new threat, hundreds of new and more deadly SS-20 nuclear missiles, capable of striking every capital in Europe. The Western alliance responded by committing itself to a counter-deployment unless the Soviets agreed to negotiate a better solution; namely, the elimination of such weapons on both sides. For many months, the Soviets refused to bargain in earnestness. As the alliance, in turn, prepared to go forward with its counter-deployment, there were difficult days—days of protests like those during my 1982 visit to this city—and the Soviets later walked away from the table.

But through it all, the alliance held firm. And I invite those who protested then—I invite those who protest today—to mark this fact: Because we remained strong, the Soviets came back to the table. And because we remained strong, today we have within reach the possibility, not merely of limiting the growth of arms, but of eliminating, for the first time, an entire class of nuclear weapons from the face of the earth.

As I speak, NATO [North Atlantic Treaty Organization] ministers are meeting in Iceland to review the progress of our proposals for eliminating these weapons. At the talks in Geneva, we have also proposed deep cuts in strategic offensive weapons. And the Western allies have likewise made far-reaching proposals to reduce the danger of conventional war and to place a total ban on chemical weapons.

While we pursue these arms reductions, I pledge to you that we will maintain the capacity to deter Soviet aggression at any level at which it might occur. And in cooperation with many of our allies, the United States is pursuing the Strategic Defense Initiative—research to base deterrence not on the threat of offensive retaliation, but on defenses that truly defend; on systems, in short, that will not target populations, but shield them. By these means we seek to increase the safety of Europe and all the world. But we must remember a crucial fact: East and West do not mistrust each other because we are armed; we are armed because we mistrust each other. And our differences are not about weapons but about liberty. When President Kennedy spoke at the City Hall those 24 years ago, freedom was encircled, Berlin was under siege. And today, despite all the pressures upon this city, Berlin stands secure in its liberty. And freedom itself is transforming the globe.

The Spread of Freedom and Economic Reform

In the Philippines, in South and Central America, democracy has been given a rebirth. Throughout the Pacific, free markets are working miracle after miracle of economic growth. In the industrialized nations, a technological revolution is taking place—a revolution marked by rapid, dramatic advances in computers and telecommunications.

In Europe, only one nation and those it controls refuse to join the community of freedom. Yet in this age of redoubled economic growth, of information and innovation, the Soviet Union faces a choice: It must make fundamental changes, or it will become obsolete.

Today thus represents a moment of hope. We in the West stand ready to cooperate with the East to promote true openness, to break down barriers that separate people, to create a safe, freer world. And surely there is no better place than Berlin, the meeting place of East and West, to make a start. Free people of Berlin: Today, as in the past, the United States stands for the strict observance and full implementation of all parts of the Four Power Agreement of 1971. Let us use this occasion, the 750th anniversary of this city, to usher in a new era, to seek a still fuller, richer life for the Berlin of the future. Together, let us maintain and develop the ties between the Federal Republic and the Western sectors of Berlin, which is permitted by the 1971 agreement.

And I invite Mr. Gorbachev: Let us work to bring the Eastern and Western parts of the city closer together, so that all the inhabitants of all Berlin can enjoy the benefits that come with life in one of the great cities of the world.

To open Berlin still further to all Europe, East and West, let us expand the vital air access to this city, finding ways of making commercial air service to Berlin more convenient, more comfortable, and more economical. We look to the day when West Berlin can become one of the chief aviation hubs in all central Europe.

With our French and British partners, the United States is prepared to help bring international meetings to Berlin. It would be only fitting for Berlin to serve as the site of United Nations meetings, or world conferences on human rights and arms control or other issues that call for international cooperation.

There is no better way to establish hope for the future than to enlighten young minds, and we would be honored to sponsor

summer youth exchanges, cultural events, and other programs
for young Berliners from the East. Our French and British
friends, I'm certain, will do the same. And it's my hope that an
authority can be found in East Berlin to sponsor visits from
young people of the Western sectors.

One final proposal, one close to my heart: Sport represents
a source of enjoyment and ennoblement, and you may have
noted that the Republic of Korea—South Korea—has offered
to permit certain events of the 1988 Olympics to take place in
the North. International sports competitions of all kinds could
take place in both parts of this city. And what better way to
demonstrate to the world the openness of this city than to offer
in some future year to hold the Olympic games here in Berlin,
East and West? In these four decades, as I have said, you
Berliners have built a great city. You've done so in spite of
threats—the Soviet attempts to impose the East-mark, the
blockade. Today the city thrives in spite of the challenges im-
plicit in the very presence of this wall. What keeps you here?
Certainly there's a great deal to be said for your fortitude, for
your defiant courage. But I believe there's something deeper,
something that involves Berlin's whole look and feel and way
of life—not mere sentiment. No one could live long in Berlin
without being completely disabused of illusions. Something instead, that has seen the difficulties of life in Berlin but chose to
accept them, that continues to build this good and proud city
in contrast to a surrounding totalitarian presence that refuses
to release human energies or aspirations. Something that
speaks with a powerful voice of affirmation, that says yes to
this city, yes to the future, yes to freedom. In a word, I would
submit that what keeps you in Berlin is love—love both profound and abiding.

The Promise of Free Berlin

Perhaps this gets to the root of the matter, to the most fundamental distinction of all between East and West. The totalitarian world produces backwardness because it does such
violence to the spirit, thwarting the human impulse to create,
to enjoy, to worship. The totalitarian world finds even sym-

bols of love and of worship an affront. Years ago, before the East Germans began rebuilding their churches, they erected a secular structure: the television tower at Alexander Platz. Virtually ever since, the authorities have been working to correct what they view as the tower's one major flaw, treating the glass sphere at the top with paints and chemicals of every kind. Yet even today when the sun strikes that sphere—that sphere that towers over all Berlin—the light makes the sign of the cross. There in Berlin, like the city itself, symbols of love, symbols of worship, cannot be suppressed.

As I looked out a moment ago from the Reichstag, that embodiment of German unity, I noticed words crudely spray-painted upon the wall, perhaps by a young Berliner: "This wall will fall. Beliefs become reality." Yes, across Europe, this wall will fall. For it cannot withstand faith; it cannot withstand truth. The wall cannot withstand freedom.

Gorbachev Astonishes the United Nations— and the World

Mikhail Gorbachev

The following selection is from a speech Soviet leader Mikhail Gorbachev gave to the UN General Assembly in New York City on December 7, 1988. The speech marked a significant change in world history, introducing a wave of transformations that swept Communist regimes from power throughout Eastern Europe over the next year and in the Soviet Union itself in 1991. Of his own accord Gorbachev promised to reduce the size of his armed forces, withdraw Soviet forces from Eastern Europe, and work toward a substantial reduction in nuclear arsenals. In this he pledged to work with the United States, the United Nations, and with any other nation or global organization in the effort to preserve peace and enhance prosperity.

By the time he gave the speech Gorbachev had already initiated major reforms in Soviet society with his movements of glasnost (openness) and perestroika (restructuring). He had also developed an effective working relationship, leading to substantial arms control discussions, with U.S. president Ronald Reagan, which he hoped to carry on with George H.W. Bush, Reagan's successor. But his announcement that he was willing to unilaterally draw down the Soviet Union's military capability, combined with his willingness to remove forces from Eastern Europe

Mikhail Gorbachev, address to the UN General Assembly, New York, December 7, 1988.

(which had been one of the causes of the Cold War in the first place), marked a new era.

Now let me turn to the most important issue of all, without which none of the problems of the coming century can be solved—disarmament.

International development and communication have been distorted by the arms race and the militarization of thought.

As you know, on January 15, 1986, the Soviet Union put forward a program of building a nuclear-weapon-free world. Translated into actual negotiating positions, it has already produced some tangible results.

Tomorrow marks the first anniversary of the signing of the INF [Intermediate-range Nuclear Forces] Treaty. I am therefore particularly pleased to note that the implementation of the Treaty—the elimination of missiles—is proceeding normally, in an atmosphere of trust and businesslike work.

A large breach has thus been made in a seemingly impenetrable wall of suspicion and animosity. We are witnessing the emergence of a new historic reality—a turning away from the principle of superarmament to the principle of reasonable defense sufficiency.

We are present at the birth of a new model of ensuring security—not through the buildup of arms, as was almost always the case in the past, but through their reduction on the basis of compromise.

The Soviet leadership has decided to demonstrate once again its readiness to reinforce this healthy process not only by words but also by deeds.

Unilateral Military Disarmament

Today, I can report to you that the Soviet Union has made a decision to reduce its armed forces.

Within the next two years their numerical strength will be reduced by 500,000 men. The numbers of conventional armaments will also be substantially reduced. This will be done unilaterally, without relation to the talks on the mandate of the Vienna meeting.

By agreement with our Warsaw Treaty allies, we have decided to withdraw by 1991 six tank divisions from the German Democratic Republic, Czechoslovakia and Hungary, and to disband them.

Assault landing troops and several other formations and units, including assault-crossing support units with their weapons and combat equipment, will also be withdrawn from the groups of Soviet forces stationed in those countries.

Soviet forces stationed in those countries will be reduced by 50,000 men and 5,000 tanks.

All Soviet divisions remaining, for the time being, in the territory of our allies are being reorganized. Their structure will be different from what it is now: a large number of tanks will be withdrawn, and they will become clearly defensive.

At the same time, we shall reduce the numerical strength of the armed forces and the numbers of armaments stationed in the European part of the USSR.

In total, Soviet armed forces in this part of our country and on the territory of our European allies will be reduced by 10,000 tanks, 8,500 artillery systems and 800 combat aircraft.

During the next two years we shall reduce significantly our armed forces in the Asian part of our country too. By agreement with the government of the Mongolian People's Republic, a major portion of Soviet troops temporarily stationed there will return home.

In taking this fundamental decision the Soviet leadership expresses the will of the people, who have undertaken a profound renewal of their entire socialist society.

We shall maintain our country's defense capability at a level of reasonable and reliable sufficiency, so that no one might be tempted to encroach on the security of the USSR or our allies.

A Call for Economic Disarmament

By all our activities in favor of demilitarizing international relations, we wish to draw the attention of the international community to yet another pressing problem—the problem of transition from the economy of armaments to an economy of disarmaments.

Is the conversion of arms protection realistic? I have already had occasion to speak about this. We think that it is indeed realistic.

The Soviet Union, for its part, is prepared:

• to draw up and make public our internal plan of conversion, in the framework of our economic reform effort;

• to prepare plans for the conversion of two or three defense plants as an experiment, during the course of 1989; and

• to make public our experience in providing employment for specialists from military industry and in using its equipment, buildings and facilities in civilian production.

We consider it desirable for all countries, especially the great military powers, to submit to the United Nations their conversion plans.

It would also be useful to set up a group of scientists to undertake a thorough analysis of the problem of conversion in depth, both in general and with regard to individual countries and regions, and report its findings to the Secretary-General of the United Nations, and subsequently, to have this matter considered at a session of the General Assembly.

And finally, since I am here on American soil, and also for other obvious reasons, I have to turn to the subject of our relations with this great country. I had a chance to appreciate the full measure of its hospitality during my memorable visit to Washington exactly a year ago.

The relations between the Soviet Union and the United States of America have a history of five and a half decades. As the world changed, so did the character, role and place of those relations in world politics.

For too long a time they were characterized by confrontation and sometimes hostility—either open or concealed.

But in the last few years the entire world could breathe a sigh of relief thanks to the change for the better in the substance and the atmosphere of the relationship between Moscow and Washington.

No one intends to underestimate the seriousness of our differences and the toughness of problems yet to be solved. We have, however, already graduated from the primary school of learning to understand each other and seek solutions in both our own and common interests.

The USSR and the United States have built the largest nuclear missile arsenals. But it is those two countries that, having managed to clearly acknowledge that responsibility, were the first to conclude a treaty on the reduction and physical elimination of a portion of their armaments, which have posed a threat to both of them and to all other nations of the world.

Both countries possess the greatest and the most sophisticated military secrets. But it is precisely those two countries that have laid a basis for and are further developing a system of mutual verification of the destruction of armaments and of the reduction and prohibition of their production.

It is those two countries that are accumulating experience for future bilateral and multilateral agreements.

We value this. We acknowledge and appreciate the contribution made by President Ronald Reagan and by the members of his administration, particularly [Secretary of State] Mr. George Schultz.

All this is our joint investment in a venture of historic importance. We must not lose this investment, or leave it idle.

The next U.S. administration, headed by President-elect George Bush, will find in us a partner who is ready—without long pauses or backtracking—to continue the dialogue in a spirit of realism, openness and goodwill, with a willingness to achieve concrete results working on the agenda which now covers the main issues of Soviet-American relations and world politics.

A Radical Call for International Cooperation

I have in mind:

• above all, consistent movement toward a treaty on a fifty percent reduction in strategic offensive arms, while preserving the ABM treaty [Antiballistic Missile Treaty of 1972];

• working out a convention on the elimination of chemical weapons—we believe that 1989 may be a decisive year in this regard;

• and negotiations on the reduction of conventional arms and armed forces in Europe.

I also have in mind economic, environmental and humanitarian problems in their broadest context.

It would be quite wrong to ascribe the positive changes in the international situation to the credit of the USSR and the United States alone.

The Soviet Union highly appreciates the major and original contribution of socialist countries in the process of creating a healthier international environment.

During the course of negotiations, we are constantly aware of the presence of other major powers, both nuclear and non-nuclear.

Many countries, including medium-sized and small ones, and, of course, the Non-Alignment Movement [nations which sided with neither the United States nor the USSR] and the intercontinental Group of Six [Argentina, Greece, India, Mexico, Sweden, and Tanzania] are playing a uniquely important constructive role.

We in Moscow are happy that an ever-increasing number of statesmen, political, party and public leaders and—I want to emphasize this—scientists, cultural figures, representatives of mass movements and various churches, and activists of the so-called "people's diplomacy," are ready to shoulder the burden of universal responsibility.

In this regard, I believe the idea of convening an Assembly of Public Organizations on a regular basis, under the auspices of the United Nations, deserves consideration.

We are not inclined to over-simplify the situation in the world.

Yes, the trend toward disarmament has been given a powerful impetus, and the process is gaining a momentum of its own. But it has not yet become irreversible.

Yes, the willingness to give up confrontation in favor of dialogue and cooperation is strongly felt. But this trend is still far from becoming a permanent feature in the practice of international regulations.

Yes, the movement toward a nonviolent world free from nuclear weapons can radically transform the political and intellectual identity of our planet. But only the first steps have been made, and even they have been met with mistrust and resistance in some influential quarters.

The legacy and the inertia of the past are still at work, and profound contradictions and the root causes of many conflicts have not yet disappeared. Another fundamental fact remains which is that a period of peace will be taking shape in the context of the existence and rivalry of the different socio-economic and political systems.

However, the aim of our efforts in the international arena, and one of the key elements of our concept of new thinking, is that this rivalry should be transformed into sensible competition with due regard for freedom of choice and a balance of interests.

Then it will even become useful and productive from the viewpoint of global development.

More and more people throughout the world—leaders as well as ordinary people—are beginning to understand this.

Boris Yeltsin Calls for Russians to Resist a Hard-Line Communist Coup

Boris Yeltsin

On August 19, 1991, a so-called gang of eight consisting of Soviet army generals, KGB (intelligence service) officials, and top government officials staged a coup in an attempt to halt the reforms of Mikhail Gorbachev and return the Soviet Union to its totalitarian past. In order to marginalize the embattled Gorbachev the gang had forced him to retreat to a Russian resort because of "illness," but the plotters had failed to reckon effectively with another leader, Boris Yeltsin. Yeltsin, the recently elected leader of the Russian Soviet Republic, had observed over the last two years the movements for freedom in Eastern Europe and in the Soviet republics inhabited by people other than ethnic Russians. He was not ready to halt the move toward greater freedom by allowing the coup's plotters, who were mostly interested in hanging on to their privileges and positions, to succeed. Already prepared to take such moves as establishing a Russian government in exile, and having already called for a general strike, Yeltsin made the speech that makes up the following selection. In a dramatic move captured by news photographers from around the world, Yeltsin climbed atop a tank in front of the White House, Russia's parliament building, and exhorted Soviet soldiers

Boris Yeltsin, appeal to the soldiers and officers of the USSR Armed Forces, the USSR Committee for State Security (KGB), and the USSR Ministry of Internal Affairs (MVD), Moscow, USSR, August 19, 1991.

to resist the coup. Yeltsin's courageous move, in part, ensured that the coup failed and helped to establish himself as the dominant Russian leader, supplanting Gorbachev. In the months after this speech, the Soviet Union was dismantled, Russia took steps toward beginning a democratic government, and the Cold War was over.

Servicemen!
Countrymen!

An attempt has been made to stage a coup d'état. The President of the country, the Commander-in-Chief of the Armed Forces of the USSR, has been removed from power. The Vice President, the Chairman of the KGB, and the First Deputy Chairman of the Defense Council [of the USSR] have formed an unconstitutional body, and have thereby committed the most serious crime against the state. The country is faced with the threat of terror. The "order" promised by the self-appointed saviors of the Fatherland will result in tragedy: wholesale repression of dissent, concentration camps, nighttime arrests. "A better life" will remain a propaganda lie. Soldiers and officers, at this tragic hour I appeal to you. Do not let yourselves be snared in the web of lies, promises, and demagogic arguments about the soldier's duty. Do not allow yourselves to become a blind weapon of the criminal will of a group of adventurers who have violated the Constitution and the laws of the USSR.

Soldiers! I appeal to you. Think about your loved ones, your friends, and your people. At this difficult hour of decision, remember that you have taken an oath of allegiance to your people, the people against whom you are being forced to turn your weapons.

A throne can be erected using bayonets, but it is not possible to sit on bayonets for long. The days of the conspirators are numbered.

Soldiers, officers, generals! An hour ago I appointed the head of the RSFSR [Russian Soviet Republic] Committee for Defense. He is your comrade-in-arms, Colonel General K.I. Kobets. I have issued a decree placing all the territorial and other organs of the Ministry of Internal Affairs, the KGB, and the Ministry of Defense [of the USSR] deployed on the territory of the RSFSR without delay under the command of the President of the Russian Federation, the Ministry of Internal Affairs of the Russian Federation, and the State Committee for Defense of the Russian Federation.

Dark clouds of terror and dictatorship have gathered over Russia. But they will not become an eternal night. Rule of law shall triumph in our land, and our long-suffering people will gain freedom. This time—for now and forever!

Soldiers, I trust that in this tragic hour you will make the right decision. The honor and the glory of Russian arms shall not turn crimson with the blood of the people.

A Call for Morality in Post–Cold War Politics

Vaclav Havel

Czechoslovakia, located between Poland and Germany in central Europe, was one of the more troublesome of the Soviet satellites in the years between 1945 and 1989, and the nation was the site of a violent Soviet crackdown against reformers seeking greater openness in 1968. One reason for Czechoslovakia's intransigence was a long tradition of cultural and political independence and sophistication. Indeed, for many decades prior to the rise of communism, the Czechoslovakian capital, Prague, was one of the cultural capitals of Europe, although the nation itself did not achieve independence until 1919. Even then the nation was a somewhat artificial creation, the combination of two unique but related peoples, the Czechs and Slovaks, who had been among the many groups seeking new national forms after the dissolution of the old Austro-Hungarian Empire in 1919. Recognizing the awkwardness of their situation, and finally free to make their own choices, the peoples peacefully voted to divide the nation in two, creating the Czech Republic and Slovakia, in January 1993.

In the 1980s Czecho-Slovak reformers eagerly seized the initiative following signs of change such as the Solidarity labor movement in Poland and the presidency of Mikhail Gorbachev in the Soviet Union. By 1989 reform parties had emerged in Czechoslovakia to challenge the local Commu-

Vaclav Havel, address to the U.S. Congress, Washington, DC, February 21, 1990.

nists and dissident groups had taken shape among artistic and scientific groups and the young. Many ordinary people were ready to take action by November 1989, when the fall of the Berlin Wall signaled that Eastern Bloc communism was ending. Student and youth groups staged huge demonstrations, leaders such as Vaclav Havel emerged, and on November 27 the nation staged a general strike in which four-fifths of the nation's workers stayed home. Communist hard-liners capitulated, and by the end of December the nation was being transformed into a liberal, free-market democracy. Havel, a dissident playwright with no political experience who had served numerous prison terms, was elected president of the new nation, which he fully recognized was in fact two nations in one, by a unanimous vote in its Federal Assembly on December 29 and was seen to personify Czechoslovakia's nonviolent "Velvet Revolution."

In the following selection, taken from a speech Havel delivered to a joint session of the U.S. Congress in February 1990, the playwright expresses his surprise at the rapid course of events as well as his hope that a moral advance, a step forward in human consciousness, will accompany the political transformation of the Eastern Bloc.

The last time I was arrested, on October 27th of last year [1989], I didn't know if it would be for two days or for two years. When the rock musician Michael Kocab told me exactly one month later that I would probably be proposed as a candidate for president, I thought it was one of his usual jokes. When, on December 10th, 1989, my actor friend Jiri Bartoska nominated me Civic Forum's presidential candidate, I thought it inconceivable that the parliament we had inherited from the previous regime would elect me.

Twelve days later, when I was unanimously elected president of my country, I had no idea that in less than two months I would be speaking to this famous and powerful assembly; that millions of people who had never heard of me would listen to my speech; and that hundreds of politicians and political scientists would study every word I say.

When I was arrested on October 27th, I was living in a country ruled by the most conservative Communist government in Europe. Our society slumbered beneath the pall of a totalitarian system. Today, less than four months later, I speak to you as the representative of a country that has started on the road to democracy, that has complete freedom of speech, that is now preparing for free elections, and that wants to create a prosperous market economy and an independent foreign policy.

It is all very strange indeed.

But I am not here to speak of myself or my feelings, or merely to talk about my country. What I have just said is a small example, drawn from what I know well, that illustrates something general and important.

We live in extraordinary times. The face of our world is changing so rapidly that none of the political speedometers we have are adequate.

We playwrights, who have to be able to cram a whole human life or historical epoch into a two-hour play, can scarcely keep up with this speed. And if it gives us problems, then imagine the trouble political scientists must have, since they spend their lives studying the realm of the probable and must have even less experience of the improbable than we dramatists. . . .

A New Democracy

As long as people are people, democracy in the full sense of the word will never be more than an ideal. One can approach it as one would a horizon, in ways that may be better or worse, but it can never be fully attained. In this sense you too are merely working towards democracy. You have thousands of problems of all kinds, as all countries do. But you have one great advantage; you have been moving towards democracy uninterruptedly for more than two hundred years, and your journey towards that horizon had never been cut short by totalitarianism. Czechs and Slovaks, despite their humanist traditions going back to the first millennium, have worked towards democracy for a mere twenty years, between the two world wars, and now for the three and a half months since November 17th [1989].

The advantage that you have over us is obvious.

The Communist version of totalitarianism has left both our nations, Czechs and Slovaks—as it has all the nations of the Soviet Union and the other countries that the Soviet Union has subjugated in its time—a legacy of countless dead, an infinite spectrum of human suffering, profound economic decline, and above all enormous human humiliation. It has brought us horrors that fortunately you have not known.

At the same time, however—unintentionally, of course—it has given us something positive: a special capacity that sometimes allows us to see a little further than someone who has not undergone this bitter experience. A person who cannot move and live an even partially normal life, because he is pinned under a boulder, has more time to think about his hopes than someone who is not trapped in this way.

What I am trying to say is this: we all have things to learn from you, from how to educate our offspring or elect our representatives to how to organize our economic life so that it will lead to prosperity, not poverty. But it needn't only be a question of the well-educated, the powerful and the wealthy offering assistance to someone who has nothing and who therefore has nothing to offer in return.

We too can offer you something: our experience and the knowledge that springs from it. This is a subject for books, many of which have been written, and many of which have yet to appear. I shall therefore limit myself to a single idea.

This specific experience I speak of has given me one great certainty: that consciousness precedes being, and not the other way around, as the Marxists claim.

For this reason, the salvation of our world can be found only in the human heart, in the power of humans to reflect, in human meekness and responsibility.

Without a global revolution in the sphere of human consciousness, nothing will change for the better in the sphere of our being as humans, and the catastrophe towards which this world is headed—be it ecological, social, demographic, or a general breakdown of civilization—will be unavoidable. If we are no longer threatened by world war, or by the danger of absurd mountains of nuclear weapons blowing up the world, this does not mean that we have finally won. This is actually far from being a final victory.

We are still a long way from the "family of man"; in fact, we seem to be receding from the ideal rather than drawing closer to it. Interests of all kinds—personal, selfish, state, national, group and, if you like, corporate—still considerably outweigh genuinely common and global concerns. We are still under the sway of the destructive and enormously arrogant belief that man is the pinnacle of creation, and not just a part of it, and that he is therefore permitted everything.

There are many who say that they are concerned not for themselves but for the cause, while it is obvious that they are out for themselves and not for the cause at all. We are still destroying the planet that was entrusted to us, along with its environment. We still close our eyes to the world's growing social, cultural and ethnic conflicts. Every once in a while we say that the anonymous megamachinery that we have created for ourselves no longer serves us but rather has enslaved us yet still we fail to do anything about it.

In other words, we still don't know how to put morality above politics, science and economics. We are still incapable of understanding that the only genuine grounding for all our actions—if they are to be moral—is responsibility. Responsibility to something higher than family, country, company, success. Responsibility to that level of being where all our actions are indelibly recorded and where they will be properly judged.

The interpreter or mediator between us and this higher authority is what is traditionally referred to as human conscience.

If I subordinate my political behavior to the imperative given me by my conscience, then I can't go far wrong. If, on the contrary, I were not guided by this voice, then not even ten presidential schools with 2,000 of the best political scientists in the world could help me.

That is why I ultimately decided, after much resistance, to accept the burden of political responsibility.

I'm not the first, nor will I be the last intellectual to do this. On the contrary, I feel that there will be more and more of them all the time. If the hope of the world lies in human consciousness, then it's clear that intellectuals cannot forever avoid their share of responsibility for the world, hiding their distaste for politics under a supposed need for independence.

It's easy to have independence on your program, leaving it to others to put that program into action. If everyone thought that way, pretty soon no one would be independent at all.

I feel that you Americans should have no difficulty understanding all this. Did not the best minds of your country, people we might call intellectuals, write your famous Declaration of Independence, your Bill of Rights, your Constitution; and didn't they—most important of all—take upon themselves the responsibility of putting these ideas into practice? The worker from Branik in Prague to whom your president referred in his State of the Union message this year is far from being the only person in Czechoslovakia, let alone the world, who is inspired by these great documents. They inspire us all. They inspire us despite the fact that they are over two hundred years old. They inspire us to be citizens.

When Thomas Jefferson wrote that "Governments are instituted among Men driving their just Powers from the Consent of the Governed," it was a simple and important act of the human spirit.

What gave meaning to that act, however, was the fact that the author backed it up with his life. It was not just his words, but his deeds as well.

I shall close by repeating what I said at the beginning: history has accelerated. I believe that once again it will be the human mind that perceives this acceleration, comprehends its shape, and transforms its own words into deeds.

CHAPTER 2

Life Under Glasnost and Perestroika

Glasnost and Perestroika: Soviet Society's Uneasy Transformation

Thomas Sancton

In 1987 the world began to take notice as the reforms of Mikhail Gorbachev, the leader of the Soviet Union since March 1985, started to take root. Facing continual opposition from an entrenched bureaucracy and from hard-line Communists, Gorbachev based his reforms on the concepts of glasnost (openness) and perestroika (restructuring). The notion of glasnost implied not only greater political openness but also freedom of discussion and debate, whether in the press or in the streets. Perestroika implied an effort to both invigorate the Soviet Union's hidebound political system and to encourage economic innovation by introducing certain free-market notions such as private enterprise, competition, and quality control, the latter being particularly important in a nation where people feared that their state-produced television sets might set their homes on fire. As a longer-term goal Gorbachev hoped to add elements of *demokratizatsiya*, or democratization, to his reforms.

The following selection is *Time* magazine reporter Thomas Sancton's account of the progress of Gorbachev's reforms, from the summer of 1987. The author noted that most changes seemed subtle and peoples' acceptance of them

Thomas Sancton, "Can He Bring It Off?" *Time*, July 17, 1987, pp. 30–39. Copyright © 1987 by Time, Inc. Reproduced by permission.

slow due to fears of greed and high prices. But he also observed that many people had high hopes for the future and that the press, notably, was beginning to vigorously exercise its new freedoms. Outside experts, meanwhile, hoped that Gorbachev's reforms would provide an opportunity for the Soviet Union to become fully part of the global economy.

Can He Bring It Off?

Slowly, tentatively, a rigid society awakes to the chilly dawn of reform.

At first glance, Moscow this summer looks much as it has for decades: office workers queuing up at street-side ice cream stands, red-kerchiefed flocks of Young Pioneers fidgeting in the mile-long line outside Lenin's Tomb, old women sweeping courtyards with twig-bundle brooms, faded red signs proclaiming VICTORY TO COMMUNISM. But beneath the capital's seedy, socialist exterior there is an unaccustomed hum of excitement. Passersby pore over posted copies of Moscow *News*, marveling at articles on (gasp!) official corruption and incompetence. Once banned abstract paintings hang at an outdoor Sunday art fair. In public parks and private living rooms, families plan futures that many believe will be better, richer, freer than ever before. To the delight of many Soviet citizens—and the dismay of others—their country is in the midst of its most dramatic transformation since the days of Stalin.

Mikhail Gorbachev's calls for *glasnost* (openness), demokratizatsiya (democratization) and *perestroika* (restructuring) have become the watch words of a bold attempt to modernize his country's creaky economic machinery and revitalize a society stultified by 70 years of totalitarian rule. In televised addresses, speeches to the party faithful and flesh-pressing public appearances—often with his handsome wife Raisa—he has spread his gospel of modernization. Translating his words into action, he is streamlining the government bureaucracy, reshuffling the military, moving reform-minded allies into the party leadership and allowing multicandidate elections at the local level. He has loosened restrictions on small-scale free enterprise and introduced the profit principle in state-owned industries. His policy of openness has encouraged the press to speak out more freely and produced an unprecedented thaw in the country's intellectual and cultural life. In the human-rights field, scores of political prisoners have been freed and the rate of Jewish emigration has been increasing—to 3,092 for the first half of this year, up sharply from last year's level but far below the peak of 51,320 in 1979.

No Democracy Yet

For all his innovations, the Soviet leader has hardly, at 56, become a convert to Western-style democracy. He rose to power through the Communist hierarchy and deeply believes in the tenets of Marx and Lenin. His goal is not to scrap that system but to save it from permanent economic decline through a series of bold, pragmatic measures. As he told a gathering of editors and propagandists in Moscow on July 10 [1987]: "We intend to make socialism stronger, not replace it with another system."

Gorbachev's rejuvenating crusade raises the question of whether he can achieve durable change without provoking insurmountable opposition from party conservatives and fearful bureaucrats. After all, Nikita Khrushchev was swept from power 23 years ago for attempting reforms far less daring than Gorbachev's. More recently, when Deng Xiaoping's economic liberalization in China began to spill over into the political sphere, hard-liners rose up and forced the ouster of reformist Communist Party Chief Hu Yaobang early this year. Even if such internal party opposition does not stop Gorbachev, how far can he push change without unleashing democratic forces that could ultimately destabilize Soviet society? Mindful of that danger, Gorbachev warned the editors and propagandists that openness "is not an attempt to undermine socialism."

Gorbachev cleared a major hurdle at last month's Central Committee plenum [meeting] when he won backing for a far-reaching new law on state enterprises. The measure is intended to loosen the stranglehold of the central planning bureaucracy by giving greater independence to factory and farm managers. Among other provisions, it will require that local managers be elected by their workers and that the country's 48,000 state enterprises fund new and continuing operations from their own profits. Before the law takes effect next January, it must be accompanied by a package of enabling legislation dealing with such things as credit and finance, technological research and an overhaul of the state-controlled pricing system.

Economic Reforms

Gorbachev had in fact prepared eleven draft decrees along those lines, but chose not to put them to a vote at the plenum. Some Western analysts took this as a sign that he had yet to overcome resistance from conservatives among the Central Committee's 307 members, 60% of whom are holdovers from the Brezhnev era [1964–1982] Gorbachev is widely expected to seek a purge of such foot draggers at a national party conference that he has scheduled for June 1988. Nonetheless, the plenum left little doubt about his political strength, which was underscored by the naming of three of his supporters to the ruling Politburo. The new appointments meant that Gorbachev allies now occupy at least half of the 14 seats on the expanded Politburo.

A Surprise Visit

Gorbachev had demonstrated his clout four weeks before the plenum by taking swift action against the military in the wake of West German Pilot Mathias Rust's spectacular landing just outside Red Square. When the Hamburg teenager's single-engine Cessna penetrated some 400 miles of Soviet airspace with impunity, Gorbachev immediately sacked Defense Minister Sergei Sokolov and Air Defense Chief Alexander Koldunov. In addition to giving the country an object lesson in the personal accountability of those in power—and demonstrating the military's subservience to the political leadership—Gorbachev seized the occasion to place a reform-minded ally, General of the Army Dmitri Yazov, 63, in the Defense Minister's job.

In the past month, and especially in the wake of the Central Committee session, Gorbachev has moved decisively in the direction of what he calls radical reform. Before the plenum, some Western analysts suspected that *perestroika* was largely a rhetorical exercise backed by a set of diluted half-measures. But Gorbachev's latest proposals, along with recent declarations by some of his key economic advisers, point to more far-reaching structural changes. Economist Abel Aganbegyan, for example, has advocated letting prices rise to market levels. At present, government subsidies on such items as food, clothing and shelter run to $114 billion a year, straining the government budget and encouraging shortages and inefficiency. Aganbegyan has also raised the possibility of closing "thousands" of unprofitable enterprises.

Similarly radical solutions were outlined by Economist Nikolai Shmelev in the June issue of *Novy Mir* (New World), a literary monthly. Lambasting inept managers for "their feudal ideology," he warned that "economics has laws that are just as terrible to violate as the laws of the atomic reactor in Chernobyl [which melted down with great destruction in 1986]." Shmelev called for the introduction of free-market mechanisms even if that meant tolerating unemployment—a concept virtually unheard of in the Soviet Union. Gorbachev later praised the article for painting a "picture close to what in fact exists," but he stressed his commitment to full employment.

Opening Dangerous Doors

Gorbachev must realize, however, that any meaningful reform of pricing and central planning will inevitably cause some inflation and unemployment. Another consequence of his proposals would be an increase in pay incentives, thus risking the creation of rich and poor in a society that has long been, for the most part, egalitarian in pay though not in perquisites. Perhaps a greater danger is that incentives may undermine the very ideological underpinnings of Communism and thus prove unworkable. Nonetheless, Gorbachev appears to be serious about that reform. As he said in his plenum speech last month, "It is particularly important that the actual pay of every worker be closely linked to his personal contribution to the end result, and that no limit be set." The Soviet leader also applied the profit principle to agriculture, calling for a sharp increase in small-scale private farming to supplement the inadequate output of the collective farms. In a departure from traditional Soviet thinking, he declared that "competition is central to activating the motive forces of socialism."

In these and other ways, the General Secretary has hurled new challenges at a nation that was temperamentally and ideologically unprepared for change. It is not surprising, therefore, that his policies have met with resistance from an entrenched party and government bureaucracy that is wary of losing its prerogatives. As Gorbachev put it in an interview with the Italian Communist Party daily *L'Unità* last May, "It is a question of old approaches, the inertia of old habits and of fear of novelty and responsibility for specific deeds. We are also being hampered by entrusted bureaucratic layers."

This opposition has no identifiable organization, leadership or platform. It includes an amorphous mass of party officials, civil servants and managers whose administrative foot dragging can stall or ultimately sabotage the reforms. Gorbachev has tightened his control over the Politburo, the party's supreme body, but he still faces formidable opposition from this large, inchoate group.

Dangerous TV Sets

Even if he enjoyed unanimous support, Gorbachev would need a rare combination of skill and luck to solve the awesome economic problems that have been accumulating for a half-century. Stalin's legacy of centralized planning, collectivized agriculture and reliance on heavy industry, while effective at first in building up the Communist economy, ultimately produced a rigid and inefficient system. Having grown dramatically during the 1930s, the Soviet economy was sputtering along at an anemic average rate of 2% by the mid-80s—lower than any other industrialized country except Britain. Agricultural output rose less than 1% a year between 1971 and 1979 because of a combination of bad weather and bad management. Industrial production has been chronically hampered by supply bottlenecks, absenteeism and equipment failures. Most Soviet industrial goods remain far below worldwide standards in quality and design. A recent article in a Moscow newspaper noted that 40%

of the 28,056 fires reported in the city last year were caused by
faulty television sets. In a 1986 speech, Gorbachev cited the example of a TV factory in Kuybyshev that turned out 49,000 de-
fective sets. Said he: "We cannot put up with such things."

Shoddy TV sets are typical of the Soviet consumer's woes.
Moscow's elephantine planning bureaucracy, which fixes production targets for more than 70,000 items and sets some
200,000 prices each year, has traditionally stinted the production of consumer goods and favored the military, heavy industry
and, with impressive results, the space program. Soviet shoppers
have long been subjected to recurring shortages of such essentials as shoes, matches, fruits and vegetables. This summer there
have even been shortages of those most common of Soviet sta-
ples, potatoes and onions. Some 20% of the country's urban
population still lives in communal apartments, where several
families must share a kitchen and a bathroom. Alcoholism and
a decline in the quality of health care contributed to an alarming
jump in the Soviet death rate, from 6.9 per 1,000 in 1964 to
10.3 in 1980 (the figure was 8.7 for the U.S. in 1980).

By the time Gorbachev came to power, the Soviet system
was desperately in need of change, and the new General Secretary was determined to bring it about. As soon as he took office, Gorbachev began preaching *perestroika*, exhorting his
fellow citizens to work harder, ordering a crackdown on alcoholism and vowing to "rap inefficient economic executives over
the knuckles." Meanwhile, he launched his *glasnost* campaign
in a bid to win the support of the intelligentsia.

Suddenly Soviet television began broadcasting frank discussions of social and economic problems. Press articles appeared
on such subjects as drug abuse and juvenile delinquency. The
picture magazine *Ogonyok* and the multilanguage weekly
Moscow *News* started printing hard-hitting stories about cor-
rupt officials, inefficient factories and alienated youth.
Ogonyok, for example, has published such long-banned writers as Vlladimir Nabokov and Osip Mandelstam. Moscow
News has exposed police harassment of a journalist seeking to
document shoddy construction of a power plant. Just how daring the press became is illustrated by a joke making the rounds

in Moscow. A pensioner calls a friend and exclaims, "Did you see that incredible article in *Pravda* [*Truth*; top Soviet newspaper] today?" "No, tell me about it," says the friend. "Sorry," the pensioner replies, "not on the phone."

Meanwhile, what is by Soviet standards a spectacular thaw has got under way in the cultural domain. During the past year more than a dozen previously banned movies have been screened before fascinated audiences. On the stage, plays like Mikhail Shatrov's *Dictatorship of Conscience* examine past failures of Communism. Anatoli Rybakov's *Children of the Arbat*, a novel that chronicles the murderous Stalinist purges of the 1930s, appeared in a literary journal after going unpublished for two decades. Last month a group of ex-political prisoners and dissident writers applied for permission to publish their own magazine, aptly titled *Glasnost*. The government has so far given no official answer, but the first issue, in the form of typed carbon copies, has been allowed to circulate freely.

A Freer Press and Stage

By providing more journalistic and cultural freedom, Gorbachev has been able to produce an immediate, highly visible burst of reform at relatively little cost. A more difficult task will be introducing more *demokratizatsiya* into the political system, though here too the Soviets have taken some tentative first steps. Late last month, for the first time since the early days of Soviet power, voters in 5% of the country's roughly 52,000 districts were allowed to choose from party-appointed electoral lists with more candidates on the ballot than positions to be filled. The Supreme Soviet, the country's nominal parliament, voted to permit popular referendums on regional political and social issues and to allow citizens the right of judicial appeal against certain decisions by Communist Party officials.

For all his cultural and political innovations, Gorbachev's greatest challenge remains the economy. He has vowed to double economic output by the year 2000, though his policies have not yet begun to produce measurable results. Some critics say the reforms proposed so far involve more tinkering than reconstruction. Still, Gorbachev has launched an impressive array of initiatives to get the economy moving while preparing the way for more structural changes.

He has created a system of factory inspectors who can reject substandard products. Discouraged by the industrial ministries' reluctance to introduce new technology, he has formed conglomerates that combine both research and production facilities. The new high-tech factories, most of them run by the Academy of Sciences instead of the ministries, will be allowed to keep part of any profits they earn. In addition, the Academy of the National Economy is functioning as a management training institute, with seminars and case-study courses similar to those at top U.S. business schools.

Corporate Responsibility

Several hundred of the 48,000 state-owned firms have already been put on a self-financing basis and have elected their own plant managers. Some 20 ministries and more than 70 large firms have been allowed to buy and sell products abroad without going through the bureaucratic bottleneck of the Foreign Trade Ministry. Part of the hard currency these firms earn from such transactions may be used to buy badly needed foreign equipment and technology. A similar strategy seems to be behind a new law permitting joint ventures with foreign companies. Under regulations adopted last January, a Western firm may hold up to a 49% interest in a venture with a Soviet company.

Gorbachev has also encouraged economic innovation in agriculture and the woefully inadequate service sector. In Moscow and Leningrad, collective farms are beginning to sell produce through their own outlets as well as through the state stores. A parallel development is the appearance of private-enterprise restaurants set up in competition with state-owned eateries. Another flirtation with free enterprise is the new "individual-labor" law that took effect last May. It legalizes a kind of small-scale service business that may be run by an individual or family. Owners of private automobiles, for example, are now allowed to use their cars as taxis during their time off from regular state jobs, and skilled workers like carpenters and plumbers can legally take on private work. The government last week reported that 137,000 of these individual enterprises have been registered nationwide. For all its liberal trappings, however, the law seems aimed less at increasing consumer services than at bringing under state control—and thus taxation—a flourishing underground economy that is clearly essential to the day-to-day functioning of society.

Encouraging Free Enterprise

The major obstacle to the spread of private enterprise, says Duke University Economist Thomas Naylor, "is not ideology but rather the lack of familiarity with market mechanisms." That shortcoming was illustrated recently by the baffled reaction of a shopkeeper in a state-owned Moscow clothing store when asked her views on the new private companies. Suppose someone wanted to produce shoes privately, she said. "Where would they get the leather or the rubber?" Such materials have always been distributed to state-run enterprises by Gossnab, the government's main supply agency. There is not yet a procedure under which a private shoemaker can purchase leather from a private tanner. Nor are there many credit institutions that would lend an individual producer money to start a business, much less provide the sort of venture capital that fuels entrepreneurship in the West. Work is currently under way to set up such structures.

The long-range effects of Gorbachev's policies are difficult to gauge. In 1986 the aggregate national income, roughly equivalent to the gross national product, increased by an impressive 4.1% (vs. 2.5% in the U.S.). Western experts attributed the rise to higher Soviet oil exports and the best grain harvest since 1958. Those are mostly short-term factors that do not reflect the fundamental changes the economy requires. With the current grain crop off to a bad start because of severe winter weather, this year's growth figure is likely to be lower.

Workers Slow to Adapt

Sustained economic improvement will be impossible unless Gorbachev can energize the apathetic Soviet masses. He has alienated many workers by demanding more discipline, harder work and better-quality output without giving them immediate benefits in return. His anti-alcohol drive has deprived the populace of a favorite pastime. "It's a vicious circle," says Marshall Goldman, a Soviet expert at Harvard University. "For workers to produce more, Gorbachev needs to offer them more consumer goods and services. Yet in order to be able to offer them more goods and services, he needs more productive workers."

Indeed, ordinary Soviet citizens appear to be generally supportive but widely skeptical of his reforms. When Sociologist Vilen Ivanov polled workers in a large plumbing-equipment factory, 62% complained that so far *perestroika* meant only more work. Conversations with workers bear out such ambivalence. "You cannot imagine how much inertia there is," says Boris, a sullen, red-faced young man who works in an aging Moscow metallurgical plant. "There are no changes at all in our factory, except that we get less money now. As soon as we became self-financing, our bonuses dropped because we weren't getting big subsidies from the state anymore. There may be reforms going on somewhere out there, but they certainly aren't here."

A Ukrainian driver similarly wrote to the Central Committee last May "We all vote yes, yes, yes for *perestroika*, but something is lacking. The desire burns inside, but when it comes out into the open it is all smoke and no fire." A woman living in a suburban Moscow housing block voices apprehension over the idea of price reform "Whenever meat is available," she says, "the price is too high. If they raise the rent on this apartment, we will not be able to afford it. The authorities cannot raise prices because the people would have even less." Some older Soviet citizens express strong reservations about changes that they feel are compromising their Communist ideals. "I don't want life to turn into a race for rubles," says a 63-year-old educational administrator. "How can they call that Communism? This democratization smells like capitalism to me."

Making Money

The new economic measures appear to have more enthusiastic backing among white-collar workers. "We've just become self-sufficient and have been promised pay increases," says a tall, well-dressed woman who works for a shoe-repair shop. "We'll be expected to do more for our money, of course, but we're all for that. I'm saving for the first time in my life." A middle-aged administrator in a Moscow carpet factory agrees that there has been visible change under Gorbachev. "People think what they're doing is more worthwhile," he says. "Russians were never given the chance to use their traditional wisdom because they were always being told what to do by bureaucrats. Now we are self-sufficient, and we feel more responsible about our work."

Whatever workers and bureaucrats may think, Gorbachev's *glasnost* has been greeted with an almost giddy euphoria by the intelligentsia. Says Yegor Yakovlev, editor of the innovative Moscow *News*: "We are hurrying, as if walking on hot coals. We want to show, print and stage all the things that were buried for decades as quickly as possible. We want to do it overnight."

That excitement is understandable. Gorbachev's reform campaign represents potentially the most wrenching transformation in the lives of Soviet citizens since World War II. But can he succeed? Many Western experts are doubtful. Predicts former U.S. Ambassador to Moscow Arthur Hartman: "Russian history will prove stronger than the modernizers. Real reform means distribution of power away from the center, away from the party. I don't think those guys will accept that voluntarily." Some students of Soviet history, noting that periods of reform have typically alternated with periods of reaction, suggest that Gorbachev's policies may proceed for a while and then be followed by a retrenchment, as his party and bureaucratic opponents organize to stymie them. Yet the Soviet leader has two things going for him: a lack of alternatives to his leadership and his image among the intelligentsia as the last best hope for reform.

Can Gorbachev Succeed?

Gorbachev may represent the West's last chance, at least in this century, of better integrating the Soviet Union into the world economy. There it would come under pressure to behave like a

Western country, competing for capital and markets, lowering the barriers to foreign investment and even making its currency convertible. "The present seems to be an unusually promising time for doing business with the Soviet Union," says Peter Reddaway, director of the Washington-based Kennan Institute for Advanced Russian Studies. A senior U.S. diplomat in Moscow agrees, saying that Gorbachev "may be for real, in the sense that he's tackling the fundamentals."

The scope of Gorbachev's reforms and the vigor with which they are being pursued indicate that they are not merely a Potemkin village of minor improvements designed for foreign consumption. Standing before the Central Committee last month, Gorbachev irrevocably put his political future on the line in favor of principles that sound like those the West has always championed: economic freedom, individual rights and private initiative.

These concepts do not mean the same in the Soviet Union as in the West, and their application will certainly remain limited by Western standards. There is cause for concern that an economically rejuvenated Soviet Union would be an even more dangerous military rival than it is now. Yet if *glasnost, demokratizatsiya* and *perestroika* result in less repressiveness and more economic security, and if that helps make the U.S.S.R. a better global citizen and the world a safer place—some very big ifs—then the West too may benefit from Gorbachev's reforms.

A British Perspective on Soviet Russia

Richard Owen

Richard Owen, the author of the following selection, served as the Moscow correspondent to the *Times* of London from June 1982 to October 1985. During those years the Soviet leadership underwent a generational change as old guard leaders Leonid Brezhnev, Yuri Andropov, and Konstantin Chernenko died and reformer Mikhail Gorbachev rose to power. Owen was more interested, however, in the day-to-day lives of ordinary Soviet citizens than in politics, as the selection indicates. He suggests that, despite signs that life in Moscow is beginning to improve from the dreariness and shortages of earlier years, reforms are halting and still have a long way to go; factories and businesses, for example, are slow to modernize. Owen cites failed attempts to enliven Moscow's restaurant scene and the fact that for many people felt-tip pens were more compelling than personal computers.

There are times in Moscow when you are brought up short by the rough edges of Soviet society, just when you thought things were getting slightly better. Take our local pizza parlour. It is just round the corner from *The Times*, near the VIP block of flats where senior Politburo [ruling council] leaders live. The pizza parlour used to be called the Crystal Café, a place—despite its name—of dingy tables and even dingier food. Then last year [1984] it had a face-lift with the help of imported Italian caterers. Suddenly there were check tablecloths, candles and a passable Italian table wine. The wine is still

Richard Owen, *Letters from Moscow, 1982–1985*. London: Victor Gollancz, Ltd., 1985.

there, but the pizzas have been reduced to one: a small, doughy object filled with cheese paste, the Russian version of *calzone*. "No mushrooms, no sausage, no tomatoes," the waiter explained with a shrug.

It is deep mid-winter, of course, and snow on snow is piled up on the memorial to Moscow's war dead visible through the steamed-up windows. But the real reason for the decline (those in the trade say) is the departure of the Italians. Under local management, the traditional Russian vices of inertia, indifference and inefficiency, which the late [Premier] Yuri Andropov used to rail against, have reasserted themselves.

Sharp Reminders of Backwardness

Visitors to Moscow are often struck by the fact that Russians are better clothed and fed than they had expected. But there are occasional sharp reminders of the huge gaps in consumer supply. A recent exhibition here on micro-computers drew vast crowds. But the massed spectators were as interested in routine office equipment such as pens and typewriter-ribbons as they were in the video games and word-processors. "It makes you think when you see a long line of people—including senior Army officers—queueing up in the hope of getting a couple of free felt-tip pens," one astonished Western exhibitor commented.

There is backwardness in heavy industry, as well as the consumer sector, as a visit to one of Moscow's leading electrical works demonstrates. The tape-recorders and door bells produced by the Kiubyshev Electrical Factory look dated, but then so do the giant transformers and reactors taking shape on the factory floor. Women in headscarves do much of the work manually. The factory is something of a showpiece, as it is part of the limited economic experiment introduced by Andropov giving managers the power to make production and investment decisions. The scheme—now being extended to encompass eighty-six Moscow plants—also links wages to output.

But the industrial system, apart from the favoured military sector, remains antiquated and burdened by over-centralization. The dilapidated Gothic red-brick structure of the Kuibyshev factory (formerly the Molotov Factory, founded in 1924) has not been renovated or re-equipped inside. The only visible computer is gathering dust in the manager's office. "We are not highly computerized," he remarks.

The Soviet leadership is constantly issuing instructions on the need to be more innovative and introduce up-to-date technologies, as well as use existing technologies, such as robotics, to full effect. The last such ukase [government order] appeared in *Pravda* [top Soviet newspaper] on 4 January, calling for "intensification of the economy" through "quickened tempo" in the use of electronic computers and automated systems "in the period to the year 2000".

Under the school reform initiated by Mr [Konstantin] Chernenko [premier from January 1954 to February 1985], Russian schoolchildren are to be taught to use micro-computers in their schools to provide the Soviet Union with a thoroughly modern new generation. But nobody has yet grasped the nettle of reform or backed the ideologically dangerous idea of a free flow of ideas to stimulate innovation.

Meanwhile an Apple or Sinclair Spectrum [early personal computers] is a futuristic toy, felt-tip pens are prized possessions, and the pizza fast-food business is going from bad to worse.

Waiting in Line for Consumer Goods

Alexander Kabakov

In 1989, when the following article was published, Mikhail Gorbachev had been in power in the Soviet Union for four years. As reporter Alexander Kabakov suggests, however, Gorbachev's attempts at perestroika, or the restructuring of the Soviet life and economy, had only barely begun with regard to the consumer economy. As they always had done under Soviet leaders, ordinary people had to line up for hours at state-run stores for even the most basic goods and services. Kabakov also describes people who have traveled to Moscow from faraway homes simply in the hopes of acquiring products they cannot find at home.

Perestroika, nonetheless, had resulted in certain unexpected changes. One was simply Kabakov's ability to publish critical reports of consumer society, ranging from individual experiences to more official accounts of the corruption bred by constant shortages. Another was corruption itself: The increasing openness of Soviet society, combined with unfulfilled demand for consumer goods, had led to increased smuggling, hoarding, and profiteering. Kabakov cites one expert who suggests that the solutions to these problems might include such aspects of a market economy as higher wages and prices set by the market rather than the state.

In GUM's [a large Moscow department store] food section people are queueing [lining up] practically at every counter.

The rules in the line are strict: "I grabbed the place next to this young man and only went off for a minute!" "We don't know, we didn't see it. Don't let her jump the line!" This is a tea line. The line of 80 people for cheese (of the one and only brand—no one seems to mind). Another queue is for cakes. . . . Aware of the general situation with meat, I head for the meat section anticipating the longest line. But there is no line for meat, as there are no lines for sausage or chickens, for the simple reason that the section is closed. Because there is nothing to sell?

Winding through a narrow gallery on the first floor is a line of nearly 300 for nighties of snythetic silk of doubtful taste and quality, made in Hungary and costing an impressive 70 roubles—a third of the average monthly pay. Those in the line are nearly all from places other than Moscow, many from the southern republics. Nighties are on sale at four different counters, with 200–300 shoppers in each line.

People in the line act as if they are being examined by a doctor: on the one hand they are ready with their emotions and complaints, on the other with the wish to remain anonymous. No one wishes to give their names and they answer questions on the run as they hurry to make new purchases.

Zinaida L., a woman of 62, came from the city of Ordzhonikidze. She has just spent more than one and a half hour queueing for two of those nighties—one a garish red and the other blue. "The red one is for my daughter, the second . . . well, I don't want it, old as I am! My daughter has a friend. If the girl doesn't like it, our next door neighbours would, perhaps. I'm retired on pension, so I am here to do some shopping. Where I live, the shops are empty."

Yet another line is for men's boots made in Romania and priced at 47 roubles. The line is 150 people long. There is no room to try on the boots, so people walk a bit aside and start swapping to get right colours or size. The place is littered with empty boxes.

Nina and Alexander G., a young couple from Nikopol. They use their vacations specially to shop in Moscow. They've just bought three pairs of boots. "They aren't quite snug and the colour is not perfect, but what can you do? A pair of boots

Consumers stand in long lines for basic necessities at GUM, a large Moscow department store.

like these would cost you 150 bucks or so on the black market in Nikopol."

Mikhail Yegorov, a militia colonel: "Queues also breed profiteering and cheating by the sales staff. To a considerable extent queues result from the deliberate actions of some sales clerks. Suffice it to say that goods worth 16 million roubles were found stacked under the counters in shops around the country in a recent militia operation. There are 15,000 criminal cases a year involving the hoarding of goods in shops. Hence the shortages. In addition to this is the operation of the mafia, which brings together those who have access to goods in short supply and those who sell them on the black market. In our recent operation we intercepted 4 tons of butter, 2 tons of sweets, 146,000 packs of Yava cigarettes, and 27,000 bottles of imported beer trucked from Moscow to Azerbaijan. Queues are also the consequences of uneven distribution: all goods in short supply are mainly sold in Moscow, hence the longest queues and the big elbow room for profiteers. It is they who benefit from turning Moscow into a 'showcase for foreigners'. There are 130 'hotbeds' of profiteering around Moscow. One of them is the Jadran shop where one can see queues of up to one thousand.

"One step to combat organized profiteering would be a change in legislation. Stiffer fines and mandatory seizure of the items of profiteering should make the trade unprofitable on purely economic grounds."

Desirable Luxuries

The longest line of nearly 500 people is for men's polar fox caps at 190 roubles each, or nearly the average monthly pay. The people are queueing inside a channel formed by militia barriers and metal goods containers. They are prepared to spend at least three hours to buy a big shaggy cap which has long become a status symbol. . . . "Are you sure you need it?" I turn to a guy of twenty who squeezed his way out of the crush. He mistakes my question: "It's all yours for 230, OK?"

Forty or so people are queueing up for the world famous denim that goes to make jeans. A man of 25 or so has bought 8 metres of this fabric at 18 roubles a metre. "My girlfriend will make jackets for herself and me. This is cheaper than buying one from a coop for 250–300 roubles. . . ."

Tatyana Korvagina, Professor and D. Sc. (Economics): "I wouldn't point to a 'conspiracy' of the decelerating forces as being at the root of today's queues. Hiding the goods and thus starting rumours that coop people have cleaned out shops is an effective tactic for sabotaging perestroika [restructuring]. But this isn't the most important thing. The old joke goes: 'A queue is a socialist approach to the counter.' There is much truth in it. A surefire formula against queues is to encourage a market economy, to go over to market prices that respond to demand, rather than fixed prices. The prospect draws vehement protests:

'Price hikes are socially unjust.' As for me, the real social injustice is the present prices at which only the nomenklautura [Soviet political elites] and trade elites can afford to freely buy things in short supply. The rest of us have to pay two or three times the retail price to profiteers. Wage-levelling should be ended, as should all economic privileges in favour of differentiated wages. High pay for efficient workers would benefit the entire society, as has been practically shown by the industrialized countries. To minimize the advantage this would give those who have grown rich operating on the black market, there should be a money reform. Money should necessarily be exchanged at work places in accordance with officially earned incomes. This should have been done in 1984. But it is not too late to do it now, as long as it is carefully planned."

GUM is a favourite haunt for tourists. There I see a group of Italians taking pictures of what baffles them: a line formed in an empty space. But any experienced Soviet would know right off: an ice-cream girl will come on the scene any minute now. Muscovites and visitors enjoy ice cream even in winter. Are they frosty? Or is it because of a lack of other opportunities to get fast food? The queue is patiently waiting. Is it there perhaps because of an ingrained patience?

A Young Russian Rejects His Country

Anonymous

Although Soviet premier Mikhail Gorbachev tried to contain the greater "openness" made possible by his policy of glasnost so that it would benefit the Communist regime, ordinary people outflanked him by taking advantage of their new freedoms by speaking out against Soviet society. The following selection, a brief letter to the editor of the Soviet mass-circulation weekly newspaper *Argumenty i Fakty* (Arguments and Facts), is a good example. The anonymous author of the letter is a teenager who has spent some time in the United States, probably as an exchange student. The experience, he indicates, has completely destroyed his faith in the Soviet system. He has not signed the letter fearing that he might stick out among his neighbors in his provincial town. But he bluntly describes himself as a "victim" of the Soviet system who plans to leave the country of his birth because of what he has learned and seen in the West.

I am a victim. I live in a provincial city, Tcherkasa, that's why I don't put my signature because, you understand, we all know one another.

Don't let our young people go to capitalist countries. Why? I had the chance to go to the United States on an exchange basis. I used to be a true patriot of our country and I turned into something really horrible. I became a human being. I think; I have my own opinions; it's a nightmare.

Ron McKay, ed., *Letters to Gorbachev: Life in Russia Through the Postbag of* Argumenty i Fakty. London: Michael Joseph, 1991. Copyright © 1991 by Ron McKay. Reproduced by permission of Penguin Books Ltd.

After what I saw in the USA it's impossible to live here. I'm not yet eighteen and I know that I won't do anything good for our society. I had a desire to serve my country but I don't have it any more. Because one person cannot change a whole system.

I sympathize with Gorbachev, but deep in my heart I am no longer a Soviet citizen and I don't care what's going on in the USSR and I don't believe in anything in this country. The question of whether we are worse off than they are doesn't bother me any more. Yes, we are worse off because we live like this.

I am a victim of what I saw and I know that I shall leave this country. It's not mine any more.

So, don't allow the young people to go to capitalist countries if you don't want to lose your future.

Russian Teenagers Speak Out

Galya et al., interviewed by Tony Parker

The following selection consists of an interview of four Russian teenagers by Tony Parker, a British writer. The four—Galya, Nika, Sergei, and Andrei—are seniors in the Soviet secondary school system and are fifteen or sixteen years old. They are both keen observers of and participants in the transformation of Russia in the last years of the Cold War.

Some of the concerns expressed by the four are those of teenagers everywhere, such as future plans and ambitions with regard to higher education, work, and family. They note changes in the Soviet Union that might affect them directly, such as the question of whether the two boys, Andrei and Sergei, might have to serve in the Russian army as almost all young men have been required to do for much of the history of the Soviet Union. The teenagers also wonder whether changes might be occurring too rapidly and hope that the "outside world," as represented by the interviewer and his audience, will not see the Soviet Union as backward in such matters as the status of women. One of them notes, in a manner that clearly suggests the uncertainty of the last years of the Soviet Union, that his generation faces a constant struggle between optimism and pessimism.

Galya: We are four pupils from Class II, which is one of the older pupils' classes, and is mainly for those who will be leaving school next year. Three of us are fifteen years of age, and Sergei is sixteen. We will tell you first who we are and what each of us hopes to do after leaving school. Then after that we

Tony Parker, *Russian Voices*. London: Jonathan Cape, 1991. Copyright © 1991 by Tony Parker. Reproduced by permission of the author c/o Rogers, Coleridge & White Ltd., 20 Powis Mews, London W11 1JN.

will give you our thoughts about some of the subjects you gave us the list of last week, and asked us to tell you our ideas about them. Sergei should speak first because he is the eldest.

Nika: And also because he is a man, and in Russian society it is customary for men to speak and give their opinions and females to hold their tongues.

Sergei: Well very well Nika, I am sure I do not mind at all if you want to speak first yourself. We must not let our visitor think we are as old-fashioned and out-of-date a country as you suggest. So yes please, you speak first.

Introducing Themselves and Their Ambitions

Nika: Very well then, I will. I am Nika, my favourite subject here at school is biology, and so when I leave I would like to go first to a college of technical education and study it further, for perhaps two or three years in such a college, and then continue with my studies in the same subject at university. I do not know yet which branch of biology I would like to specialise in, but I think in fact possibly it might be plant-biology research.

Andrei: I am Andrei, I am fifteen, and when I leave this school I would like to go to a pedagological institute and be a teacher-training student. I have talked about it with some of the teachers here, and all of them said the same thing, that it is good to be a teacher and they themselves enjoy it. I would not necessarily want to come back and be a teacher at this school: it is something I have not yet made a decision about. That I would like to be a teacher is as far as I have got up to now in thinking about it.

Galya: I would like very much to study law when I leave this school, but I do not yet know if it will be possible because there are certain preliminary examinations to pass first, and I may not do well at them. But that is what I would like to do if I could; and also of course I would like to get married and have a home and one child at least.

Concerns About Joining the Army

Sergei: And now I will be the last one to speak, to show you that it is not true that it is men who always speak first. My own favourite subjects here are economics and international affairs and history. I would like to stay as long as I can as a student, and go to university. But for all young men of my age there is the problem of having conscription in our country and going to the Army: you do not know whether you should get your two years' service over as soon as you can, and then go on with your education, whether you should interrupt your education for two years in the middle of it, or whether you should try to postpone going to the Army until the end of your studies. As I have said, it is a problem for everyone of my age.

Nika: Perhaps before long there will not be conscription any more, and the law will be altered so that those who do not want to go to the Army are free to choose. It is ridiculous that we have such a large army anyway. I think we do not need it at all, or at least not in such a great size as we have.

Galya: I think this subject of conscription was not something you put on the list of things you would like us to talk about, and of course it concerns Sergei and Andrei but not Nika and me. The subjects on the list which do concern us all are, in the first instance, where you have asked us to say what we think will be the most important problems facing our country during our own future lifetimes. Each of us has something to say about it.

Sergei: To me the biggest problem we have to face is the desire which is growing all the time in nearly every individual state in the USSR, for them to break away from the Soviet Union. Many of them are demanding independence immediately, and this is going to be a most difficult problem both for them and for the country as a whole. You cannot just say to the Baltic states such as Latvia, Lithuania and Estonia 'Here is your independence, take it and enjoy it.' All their economy depends upon their trade within the Soviet Union: they depend on it to provide them with essentials such as fuel, power and raw materials—and they depend on it to buy the goods that they themselves produce.

The Breakup of the Soviet Union

Nika: Before long the whole country will be having a big economic crisis because of this, and so I agree this is probably the most important problem that is likely to face us. Not just the Baltic states but nearly all of the others too in the Union, they have been under the power of the central government to such an extent they have never developed their own realistic economy. I wish some way could be found so that they would have their own government and the freedoms they want without suffering economically. But I think there are many hot-headed people both there in the different states, and here in central government, who are going to make it difficult for it to happen.

Galya: There is a possibility that violence and even civil war could occur because of it. It is important that those in power on both sides should take a wide view and try to reach compromises rather than defeat one another. And another important part of this matter is that because in all their lifetime the peoples of these states have never had freedom and independence, when they get it they will not know how to deal with it properly. Independence means not just freedom for you, but you giving freedom to other people to do what they like too, so I hope people will be tolerant with each other.

Sergei: It is very interesting for me, and I think for many other people too, to see what is happening at exactly the same time in both eastern Europe and in western Europe. It is two absolutely opposite things. In the East many of the republics of the USSR—and as well what were called the Eastern bloc countries—they are all determined to become independent. And just at the same time in the West, all those different countries are trying to come together into one great united European country. Perhaps both sides will learn from each other the difficulties and problems of trying to go in these opposite directions.

Environmental Concerns

Andrei: There is also another problem which I think will grow in size during our lifetimes, as well as this one which we have just been talking of. It is that of the increasing damage which is being done all over the world to the environment. I think people are becoming aware more and more that it is happening, and that we should try to stop it. But matters that we hear constantly about on television, or read about in maga-zines—such as the destruction of rain forests, the ozone layer, the number of now-endangered species of animals and plants, the pollution by chemicals of seas and rivers and lakes, acid rain and many other things—these are all doing great harm to our environment. We are only just beginning to learn how, and to what degree; and I think there are many cases where we have not even yet woken up to what we are doing. Also our governments will not give us full information about their activities. They are keeping many secrets from us about the way they themselves are causing damage, so it is difficult for steps to be taken to stop them doing these things. I read not long ago about an organisation called 'Greenpeace'. It tries to take action against such things as polluting the oceans with waste matter from nuclear power, or stopping the killing of whales on a huge scale for commercial purposes, and making many other protests of this sort. But it is only a tiny organi-sation and its opponents such as governments and industrial-ists have enormous financial resources. So it does not have much power to bring about change. I think these ecological problems are the ones which are going to be the most diffi-cult for us in the future.

Women and Men

Nika: My choice of subject as the most important one we shall have to deal with in our own future lives is—or I hope it will be—the question of how we are going to handle the question of the place of women in society. In USSR we are very back-ward about this indeed in our attitudes, and we must try to do something about it. Even in the West, according to magazine articles I have read, there is still much progress which needs making. A lot of women are looked upon as no more than slaves and servants, whose only purpose is to marry, raise a family, look after their husband and home, and be content with that for the rest of their lives.

Sergei: That is what a lot of women want to do with their lives, they are very happy and contented that their life should be like that and they do not want anything more.

Nika: Yes of course: it is women themselves who contribute to the problem by thinking like that.

Sergei: But if they are happy to do it, why should someone come along and tell them they shouldn't be happy, they should be unhappy about it?

Galya: Well, I would be happy to do that myself so long as I had a husband who loved me and I loved him. But I would not want to do only that, I would like to do my own work and have my own job as well. I think a problem connected with this is that many men and women get married when they are much too young, perhaps only nineteen or twenty, and then after a few years they find they do not love each other any more, and we have many divorces.

Andrei: But there is a problem too that if two people love each other and want to be together all the time, they cannot find somewhere to live unless they are married. So this means they have to get married to find out if they are suitable for each other. I have read that in the West it is not uncommon for young men and women to live in the same apartment together without being married. But if you would want to do that here, you would not get an apartment allocated to you.

Nika: In most cases a girl's parents would not allow her to live with her boyfriend, who she wasn't married to, in their apartment. So this is another reason why I say the question of women's position is such an important one: a young woman should have the right to choose whether she gets married to the man she likes, or not.

Galya: And finally all of us together think that a very important problem which faces us now in our everyday lives will have passed in a few years' time, by the time we are adults. We hope that it will have been solved, but we are also all agreed that it may not have been. This is the problem of the great shortages of food and other things in our shops. It would be very depressing for us to feel that such a problem was still going to be with us when we are adult.

Sergei: We will try to be optimistic. But I think in our hearts we are not, we are pessimistic.

CHAPTER 3

The Iron Curtain Comes Down

"Is It Possible?"

Michael Meyer, Daniel Pedersen, and Karen Breslau

The following article appeared in the *Newsweek* issue following the fall of the Berlin Wall, the event which more than any other symbolized the end of the Cold War. In it *Newsweek* reporters interview disbelieving Berliners who find, suddenly and unexpectedly, that the barrier which has divided their city since 1961 has suddenly become irrelevant. Description of the spontaneous celebrations occurring across the city captures the mood of optimism.

The Berlin Wall was built by the Communist East German government, with the full approval of Soviet leader Nikita Khrushchev, in 1961. Its purpose was to stop the exodus of people from Communist Eastern Europe into the free West: According to post–World War II agreements, Berlin, the former imperial capital of Germany, was divided in two, just as the nation of Germany had been. Berlin lay, however, entirely with East Germany and therefore West Berlin served as an island of freedom within the Soviet bloc or, alternatively, as a window through which people could escape. The wall effectively closed the window and simultaneously symbolized Communist-style oppression and intolerance. Limited passage through the wall was allowed only at such gateways as "Checkpoint Charlie." On the western side the wall came to be covered with graffiti, much of which testified to the injustices it represented. On the eastern side the wall could barely be approached at all due to the presence of border guards and a no-passage buffer zone.

Major openings began to appear in the Iron Curtain in the summer of 1989 when Communist Hungary and free Austria relaxed their border restrictions. Over the next months East German leader Erich Honecker tried to prevent their citizens from leaving via Hungary but, notably, Soviet reformist leader Mikhail Gorbachev refused to supply either help or support. At the end of October, Honecker was forced from power and the East Germans gave permission to open the borders. With the floodgates opened, the Berlin Wall toppled on November 10, as people danced atop some sections and pounded others with hammers and clubs.

The folk song's German name roughly translates as "Such a Beautiful Day Should Last Forever." The tune is sung at soccer matches and on birthdays. In Berlin last week, just after the gate swung open to freedom, it was sung everywhere— atop the wall, in the crossing points, up and down the boulevards of a city whose people had been divided for 28 cold-war years. Suddenly West Berlin blazed with neon, fireworks—and emotion. On the Kurfürstendamm, West Berlin's fashionable shopping boulevard, BMWs mingled with East Berlin's tiny Trabants, as West Berliners lining the street pounded the tops of visiting cars in triumphant welcome.

Lothar Hoffmann, 33, came by foot from East Berlin, walking three hours to reach the euphoria on the "Ku'damm." "The wall is broken," he exclaimed. "Hey, babe, it's beautiful!" Karin Tittmann admired the Ku'damm's shops and glowing signs. "There is so much color," she marveled, "so much light."

By 9:15 P.M. phone lines between the two halves of the city were overwhelmed. The number of lines between West and East Berlin has long been limited to 200—inadequate on ordinary days. And this was a day one West German radio station described as "Christmas, New Year's and Easter rolled into one." "Forget it," said Hans Mischnit, an operator at the Bristol Hotel Kempinski in West Berlin. "It's impossible tonight." But what couldn't be done by telephone could now be done by car and by foot.

"*Spassvogel!*" exclaimed West Berlin taxi driver Ermfried Prochnow, unable to believe the news and convinced some "funny bird" was trying to deceive him. The border would open eventually, he said during a drive toward Checkpoint Charlie, but not for five or 25 years. Prochnow became progressively less confident, however, as traffic began to slow. "Is it possible?" he asked, amazed. Five minutes later Prochnow turned onto a street jammed with confirming evidence: hundreds of revelers approaching the wall. "A traffic jam!" exulted the cabby, who had fled from the East a year before the wall was built. "It's a perfect, beautiful traffic jam!"

That crush quickly blossomed into a national celebration, East and West. At the Brandenburg Gate, on the eastern side of the wall, thousands burst into the old square that was once the heart of an undivided Berlin and a united Germany. East Berliners scaled metal fences and forced their way into the no man's land that had been closed to the public for decades. West Berliners clambered over the 10-foot wall and dropped into the arms of those below. East German border police watched, first with detached amusement, and then with undisguised glee. A dozen Western TV crews besieged a group of East German policemen. "Are you happy?" shouted a reporter. A young guard broke into an enormous grin—then turned his back to hide it. Nearby, a young man beat on the wall with a hammer and handed out fragments to the crowd. "The wall is gone!" the people chanted deliriously. "The wall is gone."

At crossing points around the city, police laughed and talked with passersby. "When we got the word," one cop cheerfully explained, "we were as surprised as everybody else." All vestiges of the totalitarian past seemed gone. No one checked identity papers; no one probed under car seats for would-be escapees, There *were* no escapees. Crowds streamed in both directions in a cross section of humanity. West Berlin punks exchanged greetings with East German pensioners. Members of gay motorcycle gangs stood shoulder to shoulder with burly factory workers from the East and the West. Parents trundled sleepy children back and forth across the border throughout the historic night.

Joyous Reports

East Germans shouted, "We'll be back," and most of them kept their promise. Some returned within hours, talking excitedly about their voyage into a suddenly brighter future. "It's fantastic!" "It's incredible!" "The eighth wonder of the world!" "I never believed I would be able to do this!" Such were the joyous reports of factory workers, doctors, garbage men and Communist Party apparatchiks. "It was wonderful," said a 22-year-old East German student "It's amazing how warmly we were greeted. We were applauded. They cried. They were just as happy as we were." Thousands more returned at dawn the next day. "I've got classes in two hours," said a student. A man rushed back over the border and headed for his office: "I don't want to be late for work."

Almost all the city joined the celebration. In a West Berlin bar that is often frequented by prostitutes, the proprietor stood alone, surrounded by bottles of Russian and Finnish vodka. The bar normally does brisk business at 1 in the morning, but now, it was deserted. "You should be elsewhere," he allowed. "The party tonight is in the streets."

An East German taxi raced down the Ku'damm at 2 A.M. with two women draped riotously across the trunk. The mood at Checkpoint Charlie was as buoyant as a soccer team that has just won a hard-fought game. As midnight approached, young West Germans stood atop planters and barricades, raising bottle after bottle of champagne to shake and spray on the thousands who had gathered to watch and to welcome. One good 15-second spray could set off 30 seconds of wild applause. So could identity papers waved high in the air. So could a bobbing civilian head, decked in the stolen olive-drab hat of an East German border guard. "The East German soldiers don't know what to do now," said West Berliner Jürgen Brown, a veteran of five protest demonstrations at the wall. "They behave a bit crazy tonight—so calm and so quiet."

New Role

The East German police seemed to relish their new role. *"Ciao,"* said an East German couple to a border guard as they headed toward the West. *"Ciao,"* he answered, snapping off a jaunty salute. At 3:30 A.M., a man raced across the border waving a freshly printed edition of the Berliner *Zeitung*. THE WALL IS GONE, proclaimed the enormous healdine. BERLIN IS BERLIN AGAIN. A border guard, whose job is normally to confiscate material from the West, reached out eagerly to see the newspaper. Curious citizens gathered around, reading it over his shoulder.

"Remember the ninth of November," shouted a middle-aged man over the roar of the jubilant crowds. It was a memorable day for Egon Krenz. The East German Communist leader told his followers the party had "learned a major lesson we won't forget": people will remain in East Germany only if they are given the freedom to leave. In fact, many East Germans crossed the border to reaffirm their hopes for change at home. "If these measures really take effect, life here will be worth living," said an East German basketball trainer. "I believe the government is sincere; three days ago I only wished for this." Others, while more skeptical, were willing to give the government a chance. According to a West Berlin spokesman, only 1,200 to 1,500 of the hundreds of thousands of East Germans who flooded across the city's borders registered as permanent residents in the first 24 hours after the travel restrictions were lifted. But Berliners on both sides of the wall kept up the pressure for reform. "Knock the wall down," they shouted. "Come on over."

And, impossible though it seemed, a bit of the wall disappeared the following day. Residents watched in amazement as police began bulldozing new crossings. Workmen were busy reopening the bricked-up entrance to the Jannowitz Bridge subway station, a former connection to the West; they were also preparing to open the gates to Glienicke Bridge, best known as a place to exchange captured spies.

Shoe Stores

The new opening would clearly be needed to handle the mobs attracted by the unaccustomed delights of the West. Thousands pressed together at the narrow passage of the Invalidenstrasse crossing Friday night, crushing one another against walls and fences. Harried border guards fought through the crowds to carry several babies to safety. "Go back! Go back!" a policeman yelled. "This is madness. You cannot get through." But the visitors pressed on. On Saturday 500,000 more entered West Berlin. Despite near-freezing weather, East Germans slept in Western subway stations, parks and doorways. Many were drunk on alcohol; others seemed drunk with freedom. They queued up in front of money-changers and banks, waiting to receive the $55 the West German government was providing each of them as "greeting money." But $55 doesn't go very far in West Berlin. Having waited since before dawn at a bank on Tauentzienstrasse, one East German walked to a shoe store across the street where he learned that the cheapest pair of sneakers would use up his entire greeting. "Eighty to 90 percent will go back," said a cabdriver, confidently pointing to East Berlin strollers out long after midnight. How, he was asked, did he know they were East Germans? "Other people," he explained, "don't look in every window."

But many East Germans were looking at another window—of hope. "We will go to West Berlin as tourists," said a middle-aged woman traveling with her husband near the Brandenburg Gate. She had no plans to leave her homeland permanently. "What good does it do to go?" she asked. "Our life is here. Besides, someone has to stay behind and change things. Everybody can't leave." What East Germans were celebrating was the exhilarating prospect of reform. "This is the place to be," said a young East Berlin woman. "There is action here. Every five hours, there is something new."

A Cold War Border Disappears

Robert Darnton

During parts of 1989 and 1990, Princeton University history professor Robert Darnton lived in Berlin, a city divided by the Cold War into two halves, a free West Berlin connected to the democratic Federal Republic of Germany (FRG) or West Germany, and a Communist East Berlin serving as the capital of the German Democratic Republic (GDR), the Soviet satellite nation known as East Germany. The division of Berlin, both symbolized and actualized by the Berlin Wall, replicated the division of the German nation and people themselves. Since the city lay entirely within the GDR, West Berlin survived as an island of freedom and prosperity reachable only by air or by crossing through GDR border points by foot, train, truck, or automobile.

In the following selection Darnton illustrates how, over time, the border crossings between the GDR and the FRG became irrelevant as the Cold War in Germany came to an end. From September 1989, when border crossings were time-consuming and even threatening, Darnton watched as it became easier and easier to move between the two nations until, by July 1990, border guards and bureaucratic procedures at the border had disappeared. The latter was a true sign of the decision, reached early in 1990, to reunite Germany into a single nation. Darnton recognized that problems would remain as the two halves of Germany were brought together but that the line that had divided them disappeared not only quickly but with a large degree of goodwill and positive intent.

Anyone who has ever done it knows the feeling—the slight tightening in the pit of the stomach, the hint of perspiration on the brow, the compulsion to avoid any suggestion of irregularity or even levity—for it is . . . serious business . . . the crossing of the border into the GDR [German Democratic Republic, or Communist East Germany] Or rather it was until the border disappeared. Of course, the border did not vanish overnight. It gradually crumbled, and the stages of its crumbling illustrate the way a regime falls apart. I distinguished four.

Before the Wall Came Down

Stage one: September 1989. When I arrived in Berlin, the border was intact. Despite the disappearance four years earlier of the mines and the rifles that fired automatically at anyone who tried to dash across no man's land, the Berlin Wall looked forbidding. It showed its ugliest face—the guard towers, the dog patrols, the scorched earth between the outer and the inner walls—when you crossed over it to enter East Berlin at the Friedrichstrasse station of the S-Bahn (Berlin's elevated municipal railway). Friedrichstrasse was the end of the line, the last stop in the West. You got out, clutching your passport, climbed down into an underground cavern, and waited in line for clearance by the border police, who manned the barrier where the East began.

Clearance often took half an hour or more. You had to pass several observation posts and surrender your passport to a succession of guards. They looked at it, looked at you, looked at the mirror placed in back of you, consulted a computer, took some mysterious notes, and eventually wave you on, always expressionless, always without exchanging any talk. If you had a suitcase, you had to turn it over for inspection. If you carried any Western books or newspapers, you had to leave them behind. You also had to exchange 15 DM [Deutsche marks, the German currency] at the official rate of one to one, whether or not you could find anything on which to spend the East marks. And when at last you thought you had reached the end of the inspecting and registering, you might be pulled out of the line for further interrogation. One friend of mine always had to undergo an interrogation because the police suspected he had friends among the GDR dissidents. Another refused to attempt a crossing because he thought the police might arrest him for spying—not that he worked for the CIA [the American Central Intelligence Agency]: he simply feared that the East Germans wanted a hostage in order to arrange a trade for one of their spies who had been captured in the West. The underground border station at Friedrichstrasse gave rise to such fantasies. In Kafkaesqué[1] fashion, you felt you must be guilty, although you didn't know your crime.

Travel by car was even worse. You could not drive around freely in the GDR; and if, after many weeks of negotiations, you received a visa to visit a specific town, you had to check in with the police and leave your passport at the hotel, which always charged outrageous prices for anyone with Western currency. Before letting you back in West Berlin, the border police made you get out of the car, searched through all your belongings, looked through the trunk, pounded the seats in order to verify that no refugee was hidden in the upholstery (the Checkpoint Charlie Museum displays a Volkswagen in which a woman had been hidden under the lining of the front seat), and ran a special mirror under the chassis to make sure no one had been strapped beneath it.

An Abrupt Transformation

Stage two: December 1989. After the opening of the Wall on November 9, the border remained intact but permeable, and the police suddenly became human. They had also been disarmed. Having carried machineguns in the 1960s, rifles in the 1970s, and hip pistols until recently, they now had no weapons at all. Because I had registered as a resident of Berlin, I could cross the border simply by showing my identity card. . . . I no longer had to exchange the 15 DM, but I still had to submit bags and packages for inspection.

One evening, a border guard reached into my shopping bag and pulled out the *Süddeutsche Zeitung*, a solid, serious daily

1. a reference to author Franz Kafka, renowned for his stories of bureaucratic manipulation

published in Munich. He held it at arm's length, making a face. "Why don't you try something more adventurous?" he asked. "Like *Neues Deutschland?*" I replied, referring to the organ of the Communist Party. "Not at all," he shot back with a laugh. "Have a look at *Junge Welt* and *Morgen* [two popular magazines]" He was recommending the new style of journalism in the GDR, which combined hard news with muckraking, much of it at the expense of the Party.

A few weeks earlier while traveling in West Germany, I drove to a different kind of border—the electrified, barbed wire "wall" that divided the two Germanys in the middle of the countryside of Lower Saxony. The barbed wire looked convincing enough as a barricade, but it seemed oddly out of place. It went against the grain of the landscape, slicing across hills that blended into one another as if the Cold War did not exist. At one point outside the little town of Hornburg in West Germany, a path led directly to a village in the GDR, not much more than a stone's throw away. The border police guarding the crossing from the East had strolled over to have a smoke and a chat with their opposite numbers in the West. None of them checked the identity cards of the peasants passing back and forth on foot. When I asked them why, they explained that everyone knew everyone in this part of the world, at least among the older generation. Villagers born after 1961 had never had any contact with their fellow Saxons on the other side of the border. But they made up for lost time after November 9. By now the East Germans had become regular customers in the Hornburg supermarket. I could see a long column of them winding their way across the brow of a hill. They were loaded down with shopping bags and looked like army ants returning with the day's booty from the consumer society that once seemed to lie on the other side of the world.

An Old Border Now Irrelevant

Stage three: March 1990. After the East German elections of March 18 made it clear that the two Germanys would unite, the border seemed to be more artificial than ever. At Friedrichstrasse, the guards waved you by with barely a glance at your papers, and the police at the border crossings for cars became downright friendly. Instead of demanding your passport, some of them politely requested you to fill out a form. It was a questionnaire designed to discover the preferences of foreigners so that the GDR could develop its tourist industry. Not only did it ask whether you spent most of your money on food, souvenirs, amusements, or gasoline; it also inquired whether you changed money illegally and, if so, how much. The police promised to respect your anonymity: they did not want to crack down on the black market, they explained, but rather to do consumer research.

By now, boat tours circulated through Berlin's canals as if the city had never been divided. Police chased criminals across no man's land as if it belonged to them. When emergency calls came from the other side of the border, rescue squads and firemen did not hesitate to dash into what had once been impenetrable, alien territory. Large parts of the Wall had been replaced by a consumer-friendly fence, and the booming trade in wall souvenirs had devastated what was left of the original structure. Even the guard houses no longer looked menacing. An East German entrepreneur had converted one of them in the outskirts of the city into a fast-food stand. Sunday strollers ate sausages beneath a Coca-Cola sign where machinegunners once kept watch over no man's land.

A Reunited City

Stage four: July 1990. After the currency and economic union went into effect, the last segments of the border disappeared from Berlin. No longer did the police wave you past the checkpoint at Friedrichstrasse; they themselves were gone, and their apparatus with them. When the S-Bahn rolled into the station, it arrived on the regular, East Berlin track, discharged its passengers, and continued on toward Alexanderplatz. Nothing was left from the Great Divide of the Cold War at places like Checkpoint Charlie, where Soviet and American tanks had once squared off, and the Glienecke Bridge, where spies were exchanged. People walked back and forth at those places, as if to prove the border's nonexistence by pacing it off with their feet. Bicyclists pedaled up and down no man's land. And the East-West traffic resumed along streets and trolley tracks that had lain unused under the Wall for twenty-nine years.

Berlin was at last united: one city! It felt odd to be able to walk or ride in any direction—as far as you liked, to Alexanderplatz or to the Polish border at Frankfurt-an der-Oder—without coming up against a political barrier. Of course, cities are not simply political units. They are organic wholes, so it would take some time for the social tissue of the two Berlins to grow together. But unification was occurring nonetheless, in all sorts of unexpected and invisible ways.

One was microbiological. Rabies had disappeared from West Berlin a decade or so after it was sealed off from East Berlin and the surrounding areas of East Germany. Foxes carrying the disease could not get past the Wall and the dogs patrolling it. But by mid-March three rabid foxes had been found dead in West Berlin. At that time there were already thirty-five openings in the Wall, and the West Berlin veterinarians decided that the only way to defend their half of the city was to innoculate all dogs in both halves with a special serum to be provided by Bonn.

Triumphs and Challenges of Reunification

There was also a moral dimension to unification. The GDR had always refused to pay reparations to Israel because it claimed that it had no share in the responsibility for the Holocaust. As soon as the new parliament convened after the March elections, it reversed that policy and agreed to pay the reparations. By acknowledging East Germany's part in the common German past, it opted for unification through the assumption of a common guilt.

On a more mundane level, the two Berlins prepared to unify by linking their underground drainage and sewage systems, sharing their sources of drinking water, and coordinating their network of canals. It was still nearly impossible to telephone from one part of the city to the other at the end of July. In fact, I had to take the subway to East Berlin in order to make a phone call to Leipzig. But the two federal governments announced a plan to integrate their phone and postal systems. Bonn was to contribute 5 billion DM toward the creation of a super-modern, pan-German telecommunications network, while doubling the number of telephones in the East.

Despite close cooperation between the major parties, East and West Berlin continued to be separate political units; and they had not merged many of their social services by August 1990. But they had removed the last obstacles to the free circulation of people, and the circulation of goods had increased to a dizzying pace, thanks to the most important measure since the opening of the Wall: the extinction of the East mark. Of course, economic union seemed certain to have negative effects on East Germany, but no one could calculate their cost. Unemployment? Inflation? Alienation? There were plenty of prophecies of doom, especially after the West German soccer team won the World Cup on July 8, and a group of nationalist skinheads celebrated by smashing store windows and bashing foreigners in Alexanderplatz.

Yet British soccer fans often behaved far worse, and for my part I saw neo-Nazism more as a specter haunting the Western imagination than as a reality threatening East Germany. When asked about the East Germans' problems in adjusting to the new economic order, I preferred to cite a different case of deviance. An hour and a half before the deadline for turning in East marks for West marks in the GDR, a man holding a pistollike instrument under his jacket entered a bank in the town of Herzfelde and ordered the cashier to fill his sack with money. She stuffed it with the day's take of East mark notes, which were waiting to be carried off to the incinerator. The robber grabbed the sack and ran. Presumably he did not discover his mistake until he stopped to count the haul. I imagined him sitting before a pile of worthless marks and cursing the West German capitalists.

Such incidents aside, the union of the two countries seemed remarkably successful by the time I left Berlin in early August. I could scarcely believe that so much had happened within one year. Physically, the city had hardly changed, yet it looked entirely different. A Gestalt [fundamental and complete] switch had taken place in the collective imagination, in the mental geography that had imposed some order on the world since 1945; 1945–1990 had been a good run for a worldview, but it was finished now. The basic division of East and West no longer made sense. It had come to an end right here in Berlin, where the sharpest line had been drawn and the border, now nearly imperceptible, once had been a question of life and death.

Czechoslovakia's Velvet Revolution Caps a Year of Miracles

William R. Doerner

For the peoples of the Soviet bloc states of Eastern Europe —Poland, Czechoslovakia, East Germany, Hungary, Bulgaria, and Romania—1989 was, as observers put it, a year of miracles. In that brief span of time, in fact in only the period from August to December, all those nations' oppressive Communist regimes were overthrown, voted out, or otherwise removed, and for the first time since the Cold War began in the late 1940s, Eastern European peoples could enjoy both personal and political freedom. In most nations the transformation was nonviolent; only in Romania was the Communist dictator Nicolae Ceausescu branded a criminal and executed by the new order.

The following selection is journalist William R. Doerner's *Time* magazine report on the so-called Velvet Revolution of Czechoslovakia of November 1989. Opening with a Prague crowd's cries for an appearance by Alexander Dubcek, hero of a 1968 pro-democracy movement, the report describes how groups of students, intellectuals, and reformers staged a remarkable, and in many ways, spontaneous wave of demonstrations that forced the resignation of the government of Communist Milos Jakes. As in the transformations of Poland, Hungary, and East Germany, Jakes could only watch as the Soviet Union refused his requests for support and aid. The report also quotes playwright Vaclav Havel, who was elected president of Czechoslovakia in late December as the culmination of this nonviolent revolution marked by clear goodwill and optimism.

"**D**ubcek! Dubcek!" Who ever expected to see the day when Alexander Dubcek, the man who first tried to give East European Communism a "human face," would return to Prague so triumphantly, or be welcomed so deliriously? Yet day after day, as the leaden skies of later autumn began turning to dusk, the crowds beneath the statue of St. Wenceslas in downtown Prague kept growing, in size and in confidence. By late last week they had swelled into the largest protests in Czechoslovakia's history: a half million chanting, shouting, horn-honking people, all bent on ousting the repressive rule of Communist Party leader Milos Jakes. They achieved their primary objective in just eight days.

On Friday, Jakes and all 13 other members of the ruling Politburo resigned en masse, admitting that they had taken insufficient measures to bring about democratic reform in the country. Within hours Jakes was replaced by Karel Urbanek, 48, party leader of the Czech republic. Urbanek played no role whatsoever in the Soviet-led invasion of Czechoslovakia in 1968, the principal condition set by opposition forces for the choice of a new party leader. But his views on reform are far from clear, and some observers saw him as a transition figure. Jubilation over Jakes' departure was further tempered by the reappointment of several hard-liners to a new nine-member Politburo and by the resignation of Prime Minister Ladislav Adamec, widely regarded as a moderate.

Political maneuvering will clearly go on for some time. A number of opposition leaders are already demanding the return of Adamec, whom they view as the key to bringing Czechoslovakia such reforms as interim power sharing with the opposition, creation of a multiparty system and curbs on police powers. By week's end Dubcek was calling for still more change. Addressing a vast throng on Saturday in Letna Plain, a parade area overlooking Prague, he said the Politburo shuffle alone "did not meet the demands of the people." The government, he added, is "telling us that the street is not the place for things to be solved, but I say the street was and is the place. The voice of the street must be heard."

A Tidal Wave of Change

Czechoslovakia now joins the astonishing avalanche of change that is overtaking Eastern Europe. Poland was the first to move, electing a non-Communist government in August. In the past six weeks, upheavals have taken place in the Hungarian, East German and Bulgarian Communist parties. Nor were events in Prague the only remarkable developments that took place last week.

In East Germany new party leader Egon Krenz mounted a campaign to live down his long association with his discredited predecessor, Erich Honecker, who is under investigation for suspected abuses of power. Struggling to hang on to his job as the party prepares for a seminal congress on Dec. 15 [1989], Krenz announced that he favored rescinding the country's constitutional guarantee of a "leading role" for the Communist Party, opening the possibility of multiparty rule.

In Moscow Soviet President Mikhail Gorbachev, who touched off the wave of change with his two-pronged program of *glasnost* and *perestroika*, greeted Polish Prime Minister Tadeusz Mazowiecki, the first non-Communist East European leader to take power since World War II. Only six months ago, Mazowiecki, who was imprisoned for a year following the declaration of martial law in 1981, was denied a visa to visit the Soviet Union. Gorbachev seemed to realize the ironies involved when Mazowiecki was ushered into the Soviet President's Kremlin study. "It may appear strange to some that I wish you success," Gorbachev said. "But we are interested that the governments and people who are close to us also have success."

One East bloc leader stood out, however, for his refusal to get in step with reforms: Rumania's Nicolae Ceausescu. At an old-fashioned Stalinist party congress, he gave no sign that he was willing to open Rumania to even a zephyr of change, much less a full-blown wind. In his opening speech Ceausescu said the Communist Party "cannot surrender its historical mission to another political force."

Longtime Rebels

The tumult in Czechoslovakia was more than two decades in the making, a very belated—but all the more heartfelt—reaction to the brutal suppression of Prague's experiment with democracy in the spring of 1968. Two weeks ago, club-wielding police reminded Czechoslovaks of that bitter crackdown when they waded into a demonstration of 15,000 young antiregime marchers near Wenceslas Square, injuring hundreds. Popular anger at being victimized once again by calculated police violence quickly spread.

On Sunday fledgling opposition groups banded together under the name Civic Forum to call for a mass protest. Night after night, huge crowds turned out—blue-jeaned students, matrons in furs and young couples pushing baby carriages, waving red-white-and-blue Czechoslovak flags, carrying banners and shouting "*Svobodu* [Freedom]!" Many of the chants that went up from the throng were unabashedly direct: "Jakes for the garbage!"

As the week progressed, bulletins indicating a mounting ground swell of support flowed into the Forum's makeshift press center. First came announcements of a nationwide university strike and a shutdown of entertainment. Then plans were laid for a two-hour general strike to show that the country's traditionally phlegmatic workers were siding with the opposition.

The spirit proved contagious. The staff of the Socialist party daily *Svobodne Slovo* (Free Word), which has been a mockery of its own name since 1968, announced that it would no longer spout the official line and would become an independent journal. Workers at the state television network threatened to close down operations unless coverage of the demonstrations was both prominent and fair. Sure enough, while still hardly objective, nightly broadcasts began carrying film clips from Wenceslas Square and shots of Catholic Primate Frantisek Cardinal Tomasek meeting with Prague's party boss.

Public Demands for Freedom

The nightly demonstrations went on unhindered as hundreds of plainclothes police, easily identifiable in their trademark polyester raincoats, watched but did not interfere. And while the possibility remained alive that the cornered regime might still try to quell the mounting protest movement with violence, the crowds grew noticeably more self-confident as the week progressed. Said a Czech journalist who had reported on the Prague Spring: "In 1968 it was a slim hope for change battling against overwhelming odds. Today this is the voice of the whole people when their time has come."

Nothing dramatized the wonder of that turnaround more than the public reappearance of Alexander Dubcek, the architect of the Prague Spring who was yanked from power in the wake of the Warsaw Pact invasion and has spent the years since then as a virtual nonperson. Now 68 and living in the city of Bratislava, Dubcek first sent a personal message to the crowds in Wenceslas Square expressing support for "all the demands of the Civic Forum, especially the resignation of all officials linked to the Soviet invasion." Then, even as a bitterly divided Central Committee was meeting to defuse the crisis on Friday, Dubcek turned up in person. From a balcony overlooking Wenceslas Square, he addressed the enormous crowd, recalling the rallying cry of his reform movement more than two decades ago. "The ideal of socialism with a human face," said Dubcek, "lives on in a new generation."

The Forum's principal demand was for the resignation of the half a dozen Politburo members who served as quisling in the wake of the 1968 invasion. Jakes was on the list for having presided over the purge of some 500,000 reformist members within the Communist Party during the following year. Also targeted: President Gustav Husak, who succeeded Dubcek as party leader in 1969. In addition, the Forum's manifesto calls for the resignation of Prague party leader Miroslave Stepan and Interior Minister Frantisek Kincl as the two officials most responsible for the police violence two weeks ago, and for a full investigation into the incident.

Ironically, one of the principal causes of Jakes' downfall was Moscow, his longtime backer. With the rest of Eastern Europe finally pursuing *perestroika*-style reforms, Gorbachev had no desire to set off for Malta [for a December 1989 summit with U.S. president George H.W. Bush] with Czechoslovakia in turmoil—or in the throes of a new crackdown. The Soviet leadership made its position plain in tense meetings with Czech leaders. Moscow's message: resolve the situation, and do it before the Malta meeting.

The Soviets Decline to Step In

Gorbachev may also have come to regard the official Soviet defense of the 1968 invasion as an important "blank spot" in his country's history and feel increasingly obliged to denounce it. Had he done so while Jakes and his cronies were still in power, Gorbachev might have undermined their sole claim to legitimacy. There seems ample reason to believe the Soviet leader was preparing to do precisely that, not because he was hankering to interfere in Czech affairs but because he saw such a denunciation as a necessary measure to get the history books straight.

Referring to Moscow's evident relief at the dramatic turn in Prague, playwright Vaclav Havel, leader of Czechoslovakia's human rights movement, said wryly, "We cannot rule out the situation that all occupiers of this country will have renounced the occupation, and only the occupied will still stand behind it." Added Havel, who is known for his absurdist dramas: "It is like something out of my own plays."

A Distinguished Past

Czechoslovakia's seething frustrations were rooted partly in a faltering economy. By East bloc standards, the country is relatively prosperous, with ample supplies of basic foodstuffs and fewer housing woes than its neighbors. But Czechoslovakia 50 years ago boasted one of Europe's strongest economies, and many residents compare their living standards not with those of East bloc neighbors but with those of the West. By that measure, Czechoslovaks concluded that their economy was backward.

Far more important than economic dissatisfaction, however, was political anger. Czechoslovakia has Eastern Europe's strongest democratic tradition, and its modern supporters argued that the country was being left behind by new experiments in Poland, Hungary and even East Germany. But if tradition served as a goad to some, it was lack of a historical memory that helped spur on others. The generation of Czechoslovaks now coming of age did not experience the trauma of the invasion—and the fear of provoking a new crackdown. Said Martin Mejstrik, a leader of the university strike: "Our parents are still frightened. We are also frightened sometimes, but we have less to lose."

Czechoslovakia also had men like Havel, who has waged a long and frustrating battle against the Communist regime, serving more than four years in jail for his pains. If anyone had suggested two weeks ago that a mass movement to overthrow Jakes would be led by him and his artistic and literary confreres, Havel would have been the first to laugh. But as the most prominent figure in Prague's rapidly coalescing opposition, Havel has rocketed to near cult status. "I am a writer and human rights activist, not a politician," insisted Havel. But as a Western diplomat in Prague put it, "Unlikely but true, he's the Lech Walesa of Prague."

Havel and his fellow intellectuals led Czechoslovakia's peaceful revolution in part because no one else was prepared to. Purges following the 1968 invasion wiped out all potential reformers within the party, and a continued hard line kept any progressive new party figures from emerging. The government also used Czechoslovakia's relative prosperity to buy off the workers, who proved reluctant, if not downright timid, about demanding change. Last week the workers listened to men like Havel and agreed to join in. Said a truck driver: "They showed us not to be afraid." That coalition of intellectuals, students and workers turned out to be an unstoppable force.

New Challenges for Eastern Europe

Adam Michnik

Political writer and journalist Adam Michnik was a prominent Polish dissident during the Cold War. A lifelong activist for human rights, Michnik was imprisoned for six years for his opposition to the Communist regime. In 1989 he founded the first independent Polish daily newspaper, *Gazeta Wyborcza*, where he remains editor in chief. He is the author of *Letters from Prison and Other Essays* and the recipient of the French PEN Club Freedom Award in 1982, the Robert F. Kennedy Human Rights Award in 1986, and the OSCE Prize for Journalism and Democracy in 1996.

Communist dictatorship of Eastern Europe may have ended with the fall of the Iron Curtain, but for Michnik it was a mistake to think that freedom would automatically bring democratic institutions and smooth reintegration into European society in countries that have no historical precedents in the democratic process or capitalism. Eastern European elections such as in Bulgaria and Romania produced winning candidates who were repackaged Communists who could be expected to govern the country according to old authoritarian standards. Elsewhere, political debate deteriorated into sloganeering and shouting matches. A market economy, too, cannot spring up spontaneously among people who have always had guaranteed jobs and medical care, even if these benefits were provided as if by wardens to prisoners in a cell. With freedom comes variety and competition, nationalism, and riotous pluralism in politics and religion and business. Eastern Europe will have to choose between "a normal European order" of managed conflicts and compromises or a new authoritarianism that clamps down on nationalism and rejects pluralist culture.

From Romania to Germany, from Tallinn to Belgrade, a major historical process—the death of communism—is taking place. The German Democratic Republic does not exist anymore as a separate state. And the former GDR will serve as the first measure of the price a post-Communist society has to pay for entering the normal European orbit. What price, moreover, will the old Federal Republic [West Germany], a normal European state with a parliamentary democracy and a market economy, pay for its absorption of a post-Communist creature? In Yugoslavia we will see a different test: whether the federation can survive without communism, and whether the nations of Yugoslavia will want to exist as a federation. (On a larger scale, we will witness the same process in the Soviet Union.)

Freedom Does Not Mean Democracy

One thing seems common to all these countries: dictatorship has been defeated and freedom has won, yet the victory of freedom has not yet meant the triumph of democracy. Democracy is something more than freedom. Democracy is freedom institutionalized, freedom submitted to the limits of the law, freedom functioning as an object of compromise between the major political forces on the scene.

We have freedom, but we still have not achieved the democratic order. That is why this freedom is so fragile. In the years of democratic opposition to communism, we supposed that the easiest thing would be to introduce changes in the economy. In fact, we thought that the march from a planned economy to a market economy would take place within the framework of the nomenklatura system [the management elites within the Communist Party, who enjoyed privileges such as luxury goods and travel], and that the market within the Communist state would explode the totalitarian structures. Only then would the time come to build the institutions of a civil society; and only at the end, with the completion of the market economy and the civil society, would the time of great political transformations finally arrive.

The opposite happened. First came the big political change, the great shock, which either broke the monopoly and the principle itself of Communist Party rule or simply pushed the Communists out of power. Then came the creation of civil society, whose institutions were created in great pain, and which had trouble negotiating the empty space of freedom. And only then, as the third moment of change, the final task was undertaken: that of transforming the totalitarian economy into a normal economy where different forms of ownership and different economic actors will live one next to the other. Today we are in a typical moment of transition. No one can say where we are headed. The people of the democratic opposition have the feeling that we won. We taste the sweetness of our victory the same way the Communists, only yesterday our prison guards, taste the bitterness of their defeat. And yet, even as we are conscious of our victory, we feel that we are, in a strange way, losing. In Bulgaria the Communists have won the parliamentary elections and will govern the country, without losing their social legitimacy. In Romania the National Salvation Front, largely dominated by people from the old Communist nomenklatura, has won. In other countries democratic institutions seem shaky, and the political horizon is cloudy. The masquerade goes on: dozens of groups and parties are created, each announces similar slogans, each accuses its adversaries of all possible sins, and each declares itself the representative of the national interest. Personal disputes are more important than disputes over values. Arguments over labels are fiercer than arguments over ideas.

All of this constitutes a real threat to the nascent democratic order. The years of Communist oppression taught us an acquired helplessness. We are helpless in our inability to articulate our interests, to defend our values, to distinguish ourselves from others, and to coexist with what is different.

Lack of Experience with a Market Economy

We all agree that we are returning to "Europe." But what does that mean? . . . The language that will be used by a culture that is ridding itself of the totalitarian corset will make use of different ideas and different obsessions than a culture that has been free of this corset for the last forty-five years. This dialogue of experiences can enrich Europe. And in this dialogue we, the people of post-Communist Europe, will be the ones who give more than we take. What we will give is the experience of living in ambiguity, the experience of living on a border.

Does the return to Europe mean also the return to a market economy? All of us know how to switch from a market economy to a planned totalitarian economy. Nobody knows how to switch from a totalitarian economy to a market economy, from a monopoly of state ownership to a plurality of economic subjects. As we say in Poland, we have to distinguish between an aquarium and fish soup. The difference, of course, is that you can make fish soup out of an aquarium, but you cannot make an aquarium out of fish soup. It is impossible to return the dead to life, yet this is precisely what we have to do. We have to do it without any historical precedents, and without individuals who know how to act in a normally functioning market, and in a society that has lost all the habits of entrepreneurial activity. The road to the market must lead through poverty and unemployment. Neither the institutions of the state nor the people themselves are psychologically prepared to struggle with reality of this sort.

The enemy of this evolution will be populism. Communism put into our heads the conviction that we are equal, that each one of us has the right to the same things. It did not matter that this very communism was betraying its own egalitarian declarations. We recalled, from Communist propaganda, that we all have the same stomachs, and that these stomachs have the right to the same stuff. We remembered that the state is supposed to guarantee us work and medical benefits, and we learned to blame the state for everything and to demand everything from the state, because the state, by assuming full power over people, assumed full responsibility. The state was like a prison warden who is empowered to keep people behind bars, but is expected to provide each one of them with a bowl of soup a day. Today all these ideas are exploding around us. And the price for the past is being paid by, among others, the government that emerged from Solidarity.

We say market, we say reprivatization. But that market has many names. If, after the dogmatic faith in the benefits of the planned economy, there comes an equally dogmatic faith in the benefits of the market, then we are in trouble. Because the market is to the economy what freedom is to democracy: a primary condition. But the market is not a self-activated mechanism that can replace the economic policy of the state and the economic activity of the people. The market has several names. We know the difference between the market as it is seen by [American economist] Milton Friedman and the market with a human face as it is perceived by, say, the leaders of Swedish social democracy.

The cult of the market will lead to the great triumph of Friedmanism. But what does it mean to be Chicago Boys [economists of Friedman's University of Chicago school] in a post-Communist country? It can mean a certain particular economic practice—that is, the determination to pursue a reform of relations of ownership. But it also can mean a glorification of egoism, a contempt for the weak and the poor, a disrespect for Christian options in defense of the most disadvantaged. In this, by the way, lies the paradox of the Solidarity movement. On the one hand, we opt for the market and for reprivatization. On the other, the upheaval in Poland was the creation of striking workers of precisely the huge industrial enterprises that are the least profitable, the ones that will have to be closed down.

Lack of Experience in Political Pluralism

The problem of the market is closely associated with the problem of political culture. We had no time and no place to learn this culture. Before the market, we are like barbarians. We respond to the threat with a conscious abdication of thinking, and a preference for social demagoguery. A populist is ready to promise everything to everyone, but is only able to jail everyone for everything once he takes power. Political culture, the ability to make different currents live side by side, implies the conviction that pluralism is a value in itself, that adversarial or conflicting attitudes enrich each other if the rules of the game are respected. Political culture is the ability to hold a dialogue, the renunciation of invective and hatred in political struggle, the staunch attempt to find compromises where the situation is complex.

Poland is a Catholic country. The overwhelming majority of Poles consider themselves Catholic. At the same time Poland is a pluralist society, where different ideas and perceptions coexist. Poles are indebted to the Catholic Church for saving their spiritual and national identity, for protecting them against Communist repression. But now the same Church finds itself in a totally new situation. It learned how to defend itself against communism, but it has not yet learned, because it had no time to learn, how to live with pluralism, how to exist in a democratic state.

The first answers that the Catholic Church in Poland has provided to the question of how to live in a pluralistic society make us wonder. What is the demand for an anti-abortion law, if not an attempt to inscribe in the penal code an approach derived directly from the Church's teachings? Every Catholic knows that abortion is murder, and one cannot blame the bishops for teaching what they have been taught. A bishop who renounces the struggle for God's law ceases to be a Catholic priest. But one may ask whether in a pluralist society God's law should be enforced by the police and the penal code. One may ask whether the protection of the unborn should be effected by means of discussion with the faithful or by means of discussion with a policeman and a prosecutor.

The same goes for the teaching of religion in schools. It was a totalitarian barbarity to forbid the bringing up of children in a Catholic way and to ban religious instruction in schools. Yet the attempt to impose religious instruction on all children, believers and non-believers, by means of a state decree, is also authoritarian. A post-Communist society, because it is post-Communist, is by nature not a particularly tolerant society. One may be permitted to ask whether the attempt to teach religion in schools will not lead to intolerance against the non-Catholic minority.

The argument that Catholicism is essentially tolerant, which is precisely what some bishops argue, does not convince

me. I know of no examples of Catholic pulpits in Poland condemning any other intolerance except the intolerance against
Catholics. Is this a repetition, then, of the situation presented
in the famous formula of [nineteenth-century French liberal
politician] Montalembert: "When I am in the minority, I demand rights for myself, because you set the rules, and when I
am in the majority, I deprive you of your rights, because I set
the rules"? Life in a pluralist society means an ability to limit
oneself, a conviction that such self-limitation is necessary, that
without it an ecumenical society (to use the pointed phrase of
[Polish writer and freedom fighter] Tadeusz Mazowiecki) cannot exist. My question is: How will our Catholic bishops man-
age to become part of a pluralist, tolerant, and ecumenical
society? By what means will the Church limit itself and respect
these limits?

The Dangerous Emergence of Nationalism

For a nascent democracy, the trap is nationalism, which has
exploded together with freedom. Nationalism is a deformed
reaction to the need for independence, a need that was violated by communism. Nationalism is a degenerate reaction,
because it rests on contempt for other cultures that is stronger
than the love for one's own.

In the time immediately after communism, nationalism is a
way of getting rid of the responsibility for communism. Look
how easy it is to say, if you are Russian, that communism in
Russia was the work of foreigners, Jews, Poles, or Latvians.
How easy it is, if you are Polish, to say that it is all the fault of
Russians, if you are Romanian to say that it is all the fault of
Hungarians, if you are Hungarian to say that it is all the fault
of Jews. Nationalism is not the idea of freedom for the individual, it is the idea of a national state: Russia for the Russians, Poland for the Poles. Nationalism means an exclusive
conception of the nation, because the enemy is first of all the
other nation, and then the cosmopolitans within one's own.

We should remember that the accusations of cosmopolitanism and nationalism were the two favorite tricks of Communist propaganda. The accusation of nationalism was provoked

by the demand for independence and national identity; the accusation of cosmopolitanism, by the demand for universal thinking and the urge for closer links with Europe. Post-Communist nationalism also abhors cosmopolitanism, because this nationalism is an articulation of a hidden fear of European normality, of European standards of tolerance and European democracy, of an order in which you have to renounce your own xenophobia, because, like stinking shoes, it is not allowed at a European table.

The Dilemma: Join Europe or Build an Independent Identity?

One should add, however, that this dilemma now faced by the societies of post-Communist Europe—to go toward Europe or to look for one's own way according to a nationalist formula—is not by any means an invented dilemma. It is a question facing all societies that are conscious of their own backwardness. The solution still awaits all of our societies. It might turn out that the return to Europe will be as difficult as it will be costly, that Europe will not want to accept its poor relatives. And the anti-European reaction will become a nationalist megalomania, a bizarre mixture of megalomania with a feeling of not being sufficiently valued.

Simply speaking, this post-Communist Europe of ours is rent by a great conflict of two spiritual cultures. One of these cultures says, Let us join Europe and let us respect European standards, while the other says, Let us go back to our own national roots and build an order according to our national particularity. They are spiritual, rather than political, camps, and they express themselves as a dispute over culture, not politics.

Post-Communist Europe has entered the second phase of its anti-totalitarian revolution. The first phase was a struggle for freedom, for the overthrow of communism. The second phase has turned into a struggle for power and revenge. Every revolution has its logic, and every one has the tendency to devour its own children. If the logic of compromise between the main political actors prevails, a democratic order will prevail. If the logic of revenge wins, we will face the hell of dictatorship.

We can choose a normal European order, a world of normal conflicts and normal human compromises, a varied world that is, because of its variety, also dangerous. Or we can choose an authoritarian state, a nationalism that rejects a pluralist culture, an order that gives up on religious tolerance, a strong quasidictatorial power that offers, as a solution to the common poverty, a populist envy and a chauvinism that distorts the human face with hatred.

Boris Yeltsin, Russia's First Post-Soviet Leader, Takes Over

Douglas Stanglin

On August 19, 1991, a group of eight hard-line Communists, including Mikhail Gorbachev's vice president and defense minister, staged an attempted takeover of the Soviet government. They announced that Gorbachev was being put on medical leave and that they were now in charge. The coup, which was by all accounts badly planned, was stopped in dramatic fashion when Boris Yeltsin, the president of the Russian republic, stepped onto a tank in front of the Russian parliament building in Moscow and urged ordinary citizens to resist. Public rallies were repeated in other cities, and the coup's leaders gave up after three days. Gorbachev, however, was unable to maintain authority in the face of Yeltsin's massive public support and because of his association with an institution rapidly becoming irrelevant: the Soviet Communist Party.

The following selection is journalist Douglas Stanglin's report from the newsmagazine *U.S. News & World Report* on Yeltsin, the hero of the hour and, by the end of 1991, the leader of the Commonwealth of Independent States (CIS). The CIS was a new, loose organization of nations which throughout the Cold War had been Soviet republics, among them Ukraine, Belarus, and the Baltic states of Estonia, Latvia, and Lithuania. At the center of the CIS was Russia, where President Yeltsin presided in January 1992 over the replacement of the Soviet Union's flag with that of the old, pre-Communist Russia. The Soviet Union had ceased to exist, and the Cold War was over.

When news of the coup attempt hit Moscow, Boris Yeltsin quickly summoned his aides to the presidential *dacha* [country house] in a birch forest near Arkhangelskoye, 20 miles southwest of the capital. When they arrived, about 6 o'clock Monday morning, they found Yeltsin already scribbling down the first draft of an appeal to the nation. Five hours later, with tanks ringing the Russian parliament building and the coup in full swing, the white-haired president of Russia, holding a sheaf of papers in his hand, clambered atop one of the armored vehicles to make his position perfectly clear: "No matter how the organizers of the coup explain their motives, they commit crimes against the people."

It was vintage Yeltsin, plunging headlong into troubled waters when few Soviet politicians dared even to test them. From inside his fifth-floor office, guarded during the crisis by 300 special troopers dressed in flak vests and armed with automatic weapons. Yeltsin personally rang up coup leader Gennadi Yanayev to berate him, according to a close aide. "Keep in mind that we do not accept you gang of bandits," Yeltsin told him on the first day of the coup. Replied a confident Yanavev: "We will keep in mind everything." Undeterred, Yeltsin chose to ratchet up the rhetoric—and the personal risk—by publicly warning that the coup leaders would be tried for treason.

Brave or Reckless?

Yeltsin's instinct for action and his refusal to play it safe are his most dominant traits—ones his detractors call reckless and dangerous but his admirers call courageous. (As a child, he lost two fingers trying to take apart a hand grenade he had stolen from a weapons stock.) But even his admirers worry that his brilliance at the barricades will fade once he returns to the tedious work of governing.

Last week, mixing bluster with defiance. Yeltsin alone kept the fragile democratic forces afloat in the early hours, and turned the tide against the coup. Pavel Voshchanov, a Yeltsin adviser who kept a loaded Kalashnikov assault rifle beside his desk throughout the ordeal, thumped the table and sneered at the play-it-safe politicians who caught "diplomatic flu" at the critical hour. "Today everyone is condemning the coup leaders," he said. "Today they are all appearing on the scene. But last Monday, there was only Yeltsin—alone."

By coolly facing down the coup, this Siberian peasant's son has become the symbol of a new Russia and the dominant force in Soviet politics. He has shattered the myth of the Communist Party's omnipotence and established himself as the rightful heir to power. But his stunning rise to the top of Soviet politics raises new worries over his unbridled ego, his Russian nationalist leanings and his shoot-from-the-hip style. In fact, some Russian deputies even think that he is reluctant to push for direct election of the federal president in order to keep popular local figures such as Leningrad's Mayor Anatoly Sobchak from grabbing a share of the political limelight.

There also is concern that Yeltsin's enhanced stature could alienate republic leaders already wary of Russia's oversized role in the union, sparking more fragmentation. Aides note with barely concealed disdain that while the three tiny Baltic States and Moldavia called Yeltsin with support on Monday, the big republics that eventually joined in waited a full 24 hours before doing so. A string of eight republican flags held aloft by a dirigible over Russia's parliament reflected the new pecking order. Russia's tricolor was first and biggest.

By week's end, Yeltsin was also first and biggest. His uncanny feel for the public mood has redefined political leadership in the Soviet Union, which has long been dominated by stodgy, aloof party hacks. Like Poland's populist, Lech Walesa, Yeltsin knows how to articulate the concerns of the crowd and to keep one step ahead of the people.

Russian Populist

As 200,000 people crowded below the sun-drenched balcony of the Russian parliament to celebrate the collapse of the coup, Yeltsin sparked upraised fists and shouts of "Yeltsin, Yeltsin" when he announced a new decree banning party cells in the military. With equal verve, he then called for a vote from the crowd on his proposal to rename that very square, still littered with wood and iron barricades, "Free Russia Square." Tens of thousands of hands shot in the air in approval. Later, as thousands of jubilant Muscovites in front of the KGB headquarters tried to tear down the statue of Felix Dzerzhinsky, founder of the Soviet secret police, Yeltsin went them one better: He *decreed* that it be pulled down. It was, four hours later.

If Yeltsin had been content to play it safe, he would probably still be back in Sverdlovsk overseeing construction workers. But his boundless energy and a can-do spirit inevitably drove him into politics in the late 1960s. In 1976, President Leonid Brezhnev picked him for the coveted post of first party secretary in the Sverdlovsk region. For nine years, the rough-hewn Yeltsin played the consummate politician, making a point of riding public transportation and often helping to bring in the potato harvest.

There were also a few blights on his record. It was on Yeltsin's watch that party bosses sent bulldozers in the middle of the night to destroy the house in Sverdlovsk where Czar Nicholas II and his family were murdered by Bolsheviks. Nervous party leaders in Moscow feared it was turning into a virtual public shrine.

But in a party filled with hacks and hangers-on, Yeltsin stood out. So when Gorbachev sought a new, energetic team in 1985, he plucked Yeltsin out of provincial obscurity to make him head of the Moscow party organization. The restless Yeltsin once again caught the public fancy by riding the Moscow subway and turning up unexpectedly at food stores to complain about shortages and the poor quality of goods. But among the Communist Party bureaucrats, he also made some powerful enemies by firing local party secretaries and railing against privileges for the party elite.

Yeltsin's impatience finally brought him into conflict with his more cautious patron, Gorbachev. Miffed by Gorbachev's refusal to defend him against critics, particularly conservative Politburo member Yegor Ligachev, Yeltsin complained at a party plenum in 1987 that Gorbachev was dragging his feet on reform. Rankled, Gorbachev shot back: "Aren't you satisfied that all Moscow revolves around you?"

Yeltsin's Clever Choices

It took courage for Yeltsin to take on the conservatives—and he paid a price. He was dumped from the Politburo and exiled to the minor post of deputy chairman of the State Construction Committee. But he fought back, running for an at-large seat for the Congress of People's Deputies in 1989. The more Gorbachev and the party tried to discredit him, the more popular he became. He won the seat with almost 90 percent of the vote, then stunned the political establishment by quitting the Communist Party, sending his popularity into the stratosphere.

Yeltsin cannily chose to build his power base in the Russian federation, outside the Kremlin and outside the party. That allowed him a chance to draw on nationalist sentiment at a time when Gorbachev was trying to hold together a disintegrating empire. At first, the Russian parliament picked him as chairman and Yeltsin had to contend with only a slim legislative majority against the conservatives. But early this year, fighting off a challenge by Gorbachev's allies to have him ousted, he turned the tables and rammed through legislation mandating a popularly elected presidency. Yeltsin won handily—even though the KGB tried to sabotage him—making him the first elected president in Russian history.

Facing Up to Gorbachev

Yeltsin has used that badge of legitimacy as a powerful weapon in his ongoing bouts with Gorbachev, who has never faced a popular electorate. But in many ways, the two men needed each other—the rough-hewn Yeltsin pitting his democratic credentials against Gorbachev's party card, while the smoother Gorbachev cast himself as the sober centrist against a wild-eyed radical. Their personal feud spawned a "war of the laws" between federal and republican legislation diametrically opposed on such issues as legalizing private property. Yeltsin also tweaked Gorbachev by convincing striking Siberian coal miners, who had ignored Gorbachev's pleas, to return to their jobs with a pledge to take over the mines in the name of Russia and to give most of the profits to the miners. It was an indication of his capacity to govern.

When Gorbachev swung to the right last winter, Yeltsin stood up to him, and when tanks rolled over Lithuanian demonstrators in January, Yeltsin rushed to the Baltics, signed a declaration backing their claim to independence and organized rallies in support. He then called on Soviet soldiers not to shoot citizens, even if ordered to. He has also come to Gorbachev's political aid, first signing a critical agreement that laid the groundwork for a draft union treaty, then rallying behind Gorbachev on the eve of his July meeting in London with Western leaders.

But now Yeltsin has broken out of the symbiotic relationship with Gorbachev to become his nation's most powerful politician—someone with the power to do things, not just block them. He, not Gorbachev, can now claim courage under fire, and his clear pre-eminence made Gorbachev's faint praise of Yeltsin in the aftermath of the coup seem both jarring and ill-advised. In a telling sign of the unmistakable shift of power, Soviet military police and KGB officers—hoping to capitalize on the abortive coup—almost immediately issued a call for a purge of high-ranking officers. They sent the appeal to Yeltsin.

1979

December: The Soviet Union occupies Kabul, the capital of Afghanistan, after months of trying to support local Communist warlords. The United States and other Western nations see the move as a revival of Soviet territorial aggression.

1980

July: As Cold War tensions mount, the United States and other Western nations boycott the Summer Olympic Games held in Moscow, the Soviet capital.

August 31: After a strike, Polish shipyard workers are granted the right to form an independent union to be known as Solidarity. They choose Lech Walesa as their leader.

November: Ronald Reagan defeats incumbent Jimmy Carter in the U.S. presidential election, partly due to support for his promises to take a strong stand against communism.

1981

December: To prevent direct Soviet intervention in Poland, the Polish army stages a coup and declares martial law. Solidarity is declared illegal and its leaders are imprisoned.

1982

June 8: In a speech before the British House of Commons, Reagan declares the Soviet Union a force of "totalitarian evil."

November: Yuri Andropov replaces Leonid Brezhnev, the long-time leader of the Soviet Union.

1983

March: Reagan calls the Soviet Union an "evil empire" in a March 8 speech to a Florida evangelical convention; on March 23 he announces the beginning of official work on the Strategic Defense Initiative, or "Star Wars," an attempt to eliminate the threat of nuclear missiles.

1984

February 13: Konstantin Chernenko replaces Andropov, who died on February 9.

November 6: Reagan is reelected in a landslide victory over Democratic candidate Walter Mondale.

December 8: Mikhail Gorbachev, a rising power within the Soviet Politburo, makes a well-received speech before the British Parliament during his first official visit to the West.

1985

March 11: Upon Chernenko's death, Gorbachev becomes the leader of the Soviet Union. He quickly initiates reforms through his dual programs of perestroika (restructuring) and glasnost (openness).

November 19–21: Reagan and Gorbachev meet for the first time at an official summit in Geneva, Switzerland.

1986

April: A major accident occurs at the Chernobyl nuclear power plant in the Soviet Union, resulting in detection of radioactive fallout on areas of Western Europe.

October 11–12: Reagan and Gorbachev meet for their second summit in Reykjavik, Iceland. There, they agree in principle to work on major reductions in nuclear weapons as well as conventional forces.

1987

July: Gorbachev announces his readiness to remove all intermediate-range nuclear missiles (INF) from the Soviet Union provided he can come to an agreement with American officials on an INF treaty.

December 8–11: Meeting for their third summit in Washington, D.C., Reagan and Gorbachev sign an INF treaty eliminating all land-based intermediate range missiles. Gorbachev's visit meanwhile inspires a popular wave of "Gorbymania" among Americans.

1988

May 27–31: Reagan and Gorbachev hold their fourth summit in Moscow. Reagan is received with great fanfare by ordinary Soviet citizens, while the leaders signal their intention to continue to cooperate on arms reduction and other matters.

December 7: Gorbachev makes a speech before the General Assembly of the United Nations in New York City, during which he announces that the Soviet Union will unilaterally reduce its forces in Eastern Europe.

1989

February: The Soviet Union withdraws the last of its forces from Afghanistan after a decade of occupation and protracted conflict that has become a Soviet quagmire.

March: The Soviet Union holds its first true elections for membership in its Council of People's Deputies.

June: Demonstrators in several cities in Communist East Germany call for greater personal freedoms and political reform. Free elections are held in Poland; candidates from the revived Solidarity movement receive a large percentage of the votes.

September 10: Communist Hungary opens its border with free Austria. A stream of Hungarian refugees soon takes advantage of the new exit routes.

October 6: Visiting Berlin, Gorbachev urges that the East German government institute reforms and refuses to intervene to stop the exodus of East Germans escaping to the West via Hungary.

October 18: In the face of continuing demonstrations, East German leader Erich Honecker is forced to step down.

October 23: The Hungarian government adopts a new constitution declaring Hungary a free and democratic state.

November 10: The Berlin Wall comes down as the East German government ends crossing restrictions on its border to free West Germany.

November 16: Bulgarian Communist leader Todor Zhivkov is forced to step aside as Bulgaria also begins the process of reform.

November 24: In Czechoslovakia, amid widespread demonstrations, the Communist government resigns and a new government is formed led by dissident playwright Vaclav Havel.

December 22: In the most violent of the transformations of Communist Eastern Europe, longtime Romanian Communist dictator Nicolae Ceausescu is taken prisoner by his armed forces; he is executed along with his wife on December 25.

December 29: Vaclav Havel is elected president of Czechoslovakia.

1990

February 1: East and West German leaders announce plans to gradually reunify the country.

March 14: The parliament of Lithuania, a formerly independent country absorbed into the Soviet Union in 1939, votes to break away from the Soviet Union. Lithuania's neighbors Latvia and Estonia soon follow suit.

May 30: Boris Yeltsin is elected president of the Russian Soviet Republic.

1991

June 15–17: At a Moscow summit meeting, Gorbachev and new U.S. president George H.W. Bush sign arms limitation agreements that had been in negotiation since the Reagan-Gorbachev Reykjavik summit. Gorbachev is disappointed, however, to find that neither the United States nor other rich nations are ready to offer the Soviet Union financial aid.

August 19: Communist hard-liners, opposed to Gorbachev's reforms and alarmed by the prospect of the breakup of the Soviet Union, stage a coup in Moscow intended to overthrow Gorbachev. The coup is stalled by Yeltsin, who calls publicly for resistance among ordinary people. Bush and others indicate to Yeltsin that they will not officially recognize any government set up by the coup's leaders.

August 23: In a joint televised speech Gorbachev and Yeltsin announce the weakening of the rule of the Soviet Communist Party, and in the process Yeltsin replaces Gorbachev, a dedicated Communist, as the leading Soviet reformer.

December 21: The Soviet Union is replaced by the Confederation of Independent States, of which Russia is the dominant member in size and power.

December 25: Gorbachev officially resigns, and the red, white, and blue flag of Russia replaces the Communist hammer and sickle over the government buildings in Moscow.

FOR FURTHER RESEARCH

Books

Neal Ascherson, ed., *The Book of Lech Walesa*. New York: Simon & Schuster, 1982.

Timothy Garton Ash, *The Polish Revolution: Solidarity*. London: Penguin, 1983.

Richard Crockatt, *The Fifty Years War: The United States and the Soviet Union in World Politics, 1941–1991*. New York: Routledge, 1994.

Robert Darnton, *Berlin Journal, 1989–1990*. New York: W.W. Norton, 1991.

Benjamin Frankel, ed., *The Cold War, 1945–1991*. 3 vols. Detroit: Gale Research, 1992.

John Lewis Gaddis, *We Now Know: Rethinking Cold War History*. Oxford, UK: Oxford University Press, 1997.

Mikhail Gorbachev, *Perestroika: New Thinking for Our Country and the World*. New York: Harper & Row, 1987.

———, *Speeches and Writings*. Oxford, UK: Pergamum, 1986.

Louis J. Halle, *The Cold War as History*. New York: Harper-Torchbooks, 1967.

William G. Hyland, *The Cold War Is Over*. New York: Times, 1990.

Ralph B. Levering, *The Cold War: A Post–Cold War History*. Arlington Heights, IL: Harlan Davidson, 1994.

Ron McKay, ed., *Letters to Gorbachev*. London: Michael Joseph, 1991.

Robert S. McNamara, *Out of the Cold*. New York: Simon & Schuster, 1989.

Adam Michnik, *Letters from Freedom*. Berkeley and Los Angeles: University of California Press, 1998.

John Mueller, *Retreat from Doomsday*. New York: Basic Books, 1989.

Tony Parker, *Russian Voices*. London: Jonathan Cape, 1991.

Ronald Reagan, *An American Life*. New York: Simon & Schuster, 1990.

David Remnick, *Lenin's Tomb: The Last Days of the Soviet Empire*. New York: Random House, 1993.

Martin Walker, *The Cold War: A History*. New York: Henry Holt, 1993.

Paul A. Winters, ed., *The Collapse of the Soviet Union*. San Diego: Greenhaven Press, 1999.

Boris Yeltsin, *The Struggle for Russia*. New York: Times, 1994.